*P*1

On the occasion of

from

Date

Church

*This book is dedicated to my mentor
and holy father in Christ:
the Right Reverend John-David Mercer Schofield.*

The Meaning and Symbols of Holy Eucharist:

A Worshipper's Guide to Holy Eucharist, with an introduction to liturgical worship in the Anglican tradition.

based primarily on
Eucharistic Prayer A
from
The 1979 Edition
of the
American
Book of Common Prayer

The Rev. Canon Van McCalister, OSV

Saint Austin's Desk
Peoria, Illinois

The Meaning and Symbols of Holy Eucharist
By McCalister, Van

Copyright (C) 2012-2016 by Van A. McCalister, II
All Rights reserved.

No part of this publication may be reproduced, stored in a retrieval system, or transmitted by any means – electronic, mechanical, photographic (photocopying), recording, or otherwise – without prior permission in writing from the author, with the exception of those portions which are in the Common Domain.

ISBN-10: 1499341008
ISBN-13: 978-1499341003

Publication Date: October 6, 2014
Revised to correct errata: October 20, 2015
Previously published as a Kindle Book: October 25, 2012

Published by: Saint Austin's Desk

Scripture quotations are from: The Holy Bible, English Standard Version (ESV) Copyright © 2001 by Crossway Bibles, a division of Good News Publishers, unless otherwise noted.

Table of Contents

Preface..1

1. **Liturgy**..3
   The Work of the People..............................3
2. **Seasons, Colors and Vestments**............10
   Advent 14
   Christmas..15
   Epiphany...16
   Lent 17
   Passion Week 20
   Easter 27
   Pentecost..33
   Ordinary Time......................................35
   Saints and Martyrs...............................38
3. **Common Symbols**.............................40
   Chi Rho..40
   Cross, Crucifix and Christus Rex........42
   Fish and Sign of the Cross...................44
   The Gospels and the Four Living Creatures...45
   Icons...49
   IHS...51
   INRI...52
   Jerusalem Cross...................................53
   Lamb of God (Agnus Dei)...................54
   Red Door..55
4. **Introduction to Holy Eucharist**..........61
   Scriptural and Historical Background...........61
   The Real Presence................................65
   How to Receive Communion..............69

5. An Instructed Eucharist..........................75
   The Word of God..77
   The Holy Communion....................................90
   The Great Thanksgiving................................92

6. Devotions..117
   Preparation for Holy Communion.................117
   Prayers for Private Devotions........................118
   Additional Prayers...134
   Private Prayers offered by the Celebrant......140

7. Anglican Identity..147
   Frequently Asked Questions about
   Anglicanism..148

APPENDICES..161
   A. The Prayer of Hippolytus...........................161
   B. Collects and Preface...................................166
   C. Praying the Daily Office.............................169
      Outline for Morning Prayer Rite II...........169

Glossary of Terms..175

Acknowledgments..182

Bibliography..184

Contact:..188

The Meaning and Symbols of Holy Eucharist

Preface

Much of my ministry has been spent on mentoring and preparing new-comers, confirmands, lay ministers, and recently ordained clergy for worship and ministry. It is my prayer that this brief book will provide the necessary "big picture" that we all need to make sense of this form of worship, we call Liturgy. These resources may be particularly useful for First Communion, Confirmation and Licensed Lay Ministry training. I have also been mindful of the "outsider" like myself, who came from a non-liturgical tradition and would have appreciated a primer to help me on my way as I fell in love with the Liturgy, even though much of it was an enigma. For those of us in that situation, the heart understood the Liturgy long before the mind did. The following essays and instructions are intended to help your mind catch up with your heart. However, there is not a wall of separation between heart and mind; they are in constant interaction with one another. Therefore, I have also intentionally framed the following instructions within an attitude of devotion, that we may draw nearer to Jesus with all our heart, soul, mind and strength.

May you be blessed in Christ,

The Reverend Canon Van McCalister, OSV

The Meaning and Symbols of Holy Eucharist

Almighty God, unto whom all hearts are open, all desires known, and from whom no secrets are hid: Cleanse the thoughts of our hearts by the inspiration of your Holy Spirit, that we may perfectly love you and worthily magnify your holy Name; through Christ our Lord. *Amen.*

CHAPTER ONE

Liturgy

Try to gather together more frequently to celebrate God's Eucharist and to praise Him.
Saint Ignatius to the Ephesians (*circa A.D. 100*)

The Work of the People

For many worshippers, the Eucharist is both familiar and mysterious. It is as familiar as is a computer to some – you know how to turn it on and run some common programs but most of what it does and how it works is a complete mystery. A more appropriate analogy might be how a complex symphony sounds to a non-musician – you know it is beautiful and you love listening to it, but you haven't the foggiest idea how the instruments are played, nor what imagery and motifs are being conveyed.

If you are like me, something like a narrated version of "Peter and the Wolf" by Prokofiev helps you to *see* the images the composer is painting. As a child, I recall how well Sterling Holloway's narration corresponded to the voices of the instruments, which made the music come alive. And, as I am sure Prokofiev intended, it made me realize that other symphonies are also filled with meaning. Because Prokofiev so brilliantly wove together music and story in a form that effortlessly teaches, the complex beauty of symphonies is more easily appreciated.

Worshipping in the ancient liturgical form may be as difficult to penetrate. It is beautiful but we would like to understand it better. The truth is, Liturgical-Sacramental worship is not as easy to access as modern Power-Point worship, and many curious visitors have found it too difficult to follow, or too obscure, and have simply given up on it. Unfortunately, some have even mistakenly equated that obscurity with meaningless repetition. While the Liturgy has some repetition, the meaning embedded in it is deep and rich.

Others are so intrigued by the mystery and the beauty, that they are drawn to worship and immerse themselves in the great Mysteries. That was my situation. I grew up in a fundamentalist denomination that believed that anything that had the appearance of Catholicism should be rejected. I don't know if anyone consciously thought that, but that was the practical outcome. Unfortunately, much of their beliefs were based on mistaken ideas about catholic worship. Sometime in my thirties, I began investigating the early catholic beliefs and practices. I discovered they were both Biblical and normative for the Church. I also discovered a depth of beauty in prayers and worship that I had not known before. During that time, I was blessed to witness an "Instructed Eucharist". During the Eucharist, the priest paused at certain moments to explain the significance of what was happening. That Instructed

The Meaning and Symbols of Holy Eucharist

Eucharist sparked an awakening in me with respect to worship, as did "Peter and the Wolf" for music, when I was a child.

A number of other people have shared a similar epiphany. So it is no surprise that the most frequent request for instruction that I receive is for an Instructed Eucharist. However, I have found that providing that instruction, while also trying to worship, is very disruptive and seems dishonoring to the Lord – as the worship takes second place to the instruction.

Worship has a meter and a flow to it that helps the worshippers to focus on God. It is like a great symphony with instruments leading the worshipper to certain crescendos. However, an Instructed Eucharist simultaneous with an actual Liturgy constantly brings the worshipper back to earth; it takes the attention away from the Lord, and focuses it on the instructor. Therefore, I began to provide a written Instructed Eucharist that would allow a person to follow along independently, without disturbing the worship. That Instructed Eucharist began as a small annotated leaflet, and eventually became the book you now hold in your hands.

The other difficulty with an Instructed Eucharist given during worship is that the instructions can only be of the briefest duration. Whereas written instruction is able to provide much more background for the theology, symbols, colors and movements, which are embedded in every moment of the Liturgy.

The Meaning and Symbols of Holy Eucharist

The goal of the Liturgy and the goal of worship is to glorify God. Ancient liturgical worship is always focused Godward. It always points to the Holy Trinity. This perspective on worship is a bright contrast to the preacher-focused, consumer oriented worship that is found in many contemporary churches. Before you become offended by that statement, please know that I am not attacking contemporary worship. I love contemporary worship music. I listen to it often, and would like to see it included more in the celebration of the Eucharist. And, I know that Christ is present in "non-liturgical" churches (*non-liturgical* is a common but misleading description: every church follows some kind of liturgy, or order of worship). I have worshiped and been blessed profoundly in some of these contemporary worship services.

Nor do I want to create the false impression that preaching is secondary. Without well-prepared biblical preaching that challenges us, liturgy becomes the object of one's faith rather than Christ Himself – liturgy becomes an idol.

What I am inviting you to consider – whether you are a Christian in the pew, or a leader in your church – is, to what extent our culture (particularly American culture) has molded your expectations for worship?

There are two factors to consider: (1) From the Reformation Movement through the Great Awakening, Protestant denominations have discarded the ancient forms of worship in protest against the Roman Catholic Church. Ironically, much of this was done out of the stated intent to return to the practices of those first Christians described in the Acts of the Apostles, and the Early Church. However, many of the reformers were not aware of the fact that the earliest Christians used a Eucharistic Liturgy. In many of the Protestant liturgies, the focus on Christ in the celebration of Holy Communion, has been eclipsed by the focus on preaching; (2) Since the introduction of television, we have become accustomed to being entertained wherever we go. We are constant consumers of entertainment. Even theme parks include monitors to entertain us while we stand in line waiting for more entertainment. People standing in lines at grocery stores are being entertained by their mutli-media phones as they wait. Entertainers are so revered, that they are afforded the honorary role of political analysts during election seasons, as if fame equated to wisdom.

These two factors have created a perceived need on the part of many church leaders to market and produce their worship service as if it were a consumer product. We want to bring people into our churches, so it is tempting to create the product that people want to purchase. There is no question that a number of people sitting in churches on Sunday, have *shopped* several churches until they found the one that made them the most "comfortable." The danger in this is that it can easily transfer the goal of worship from glorifying God, to pleasing the people in the pews.

A number of church leaders now study marketing, social theory, and organizational development as a way to increase membership. That isn't necessarily bad – in fact, I have a degree in organizational development, and it is very helpful at times. However, when we employ these tools in our ministries and our worship, the central question must be, "How does this glorify God?" We need to be intentional to guard against the temptation to merely satisfy a public hungry for entertainment.

Christians who are not leading worship, should examine their hearts to ask what their reasons are for going to a church service. Is it to be entertained, or is it to worship God? How much does consumerism effect your attitude toward worship? How might you encourage your worship leaders to glorify God, rather than to provide entertainment? Are your hymns person-focused, or God-focused? (For example, what is the difference between "Onward Christian Soldiers" and "Hark the Herald Angels Sing"? One is a marching song to rouse the people of God to action; the other praises God's glory.)

The word Liturgy is a combination of two Greek words: *laos* and *ergos*. *Laos* means *people* and is the word from which *laity* originates. *Ergos* refers to *energy*, and is seen in the word *ergonomic* (the economic use of energy). Literally, *liturgy* means "work of the people" and has come to mean the public expression of people in worship – the way people express themselves in worship. More specifically, *The Liturgy* refers to the celebration of Holy Eucharist. As Christians we have the responsibility, not only to ensure that the Word of God is faithfully preached from the pulpit [Acts 17:11], but also to ensure that worship glorifies God [1 Corinthians 10.31].

☩

The Meaning and Symbols of Holy Eucharist

Let the words of my mouth and the meditation of my heart be acceptable in your sight, O Lord my strength and my Redeemer.

The season now warns us to speak of the Mysteries, and to set forth the purport of the sacraments, which if we had thought it well to teach before baptism to those who were not yet initiated, we should be considered rather to have betrayed than to have portrayed the Mysteries. And then, too, another reason is that the light itself of the Mysteries will shed itself with more effect upon those who are expecting they know not what, than if any discourse had come beforehand.

Saint Ambrose – *The Sacred Mysteries*

CHAPTER TWO

Seasons, Colors and Vestments

Thus it was necessary for the copies of the heavenly things to be purified with these rites, but the heavenly things themselves with better sacrifices than these.

Hebrews 9:23

When I was nine years old two things happened that determined the course of my life: I was baptized, and I decided I was going to become a professional artist. There was no connection in my mind between those two decisions. In fact, as I grew older, those two decisions increasingly seemed to be at odds with one another. The more that my love for artwork and my skills in producing it increased, the more aware I became of my denomination's disdain for beauty. Twenty five years later when I experienced a Eucharistic celebration in a grand old Anglican church, I realized that God loves beauty! For a young man who loved beauty, but grew up in a church that eschewed all expressions of beauty, that was an amazingly liberating moment. But it was much more than simply a cathartic experience, it was insight into the very heart of the Creator. I had grown up in a Christian environment that over-emphasized a cognitive relationship with God, and then discovered that I could have a relationship with God that involved all of my senses and emotions.

This reminds me of my mother's description of how it felt to see the Wizard of Oz as a child. She had never seen a color movie, and so went to the theater expecting a black and white movie. And of course the movie opens in black and white in Kansas, but when Dorothy opens the door of her home transported to Oz, everything is in brilliant Technicolor! It took my mother's breath away. This is how the Liturgy affected me.

As a child I was taught that instrumental music, religious symbols, and rote prayers were not biblical. However, the Bible presents just the opposite case. The Bible is full of references to instrumental music, musicians, artisans, symbolism, and liturgy.

For example, consider this passage from Exodus 31:1-5

The Lord said to Moses, "See, I have called by name Bezalel the son of Uri, son of Hur, of the tribe of Judah, and I have filled him with the spirit of God, with ability and intelligence, with knowledge and all craftsmanship, to devise artistic designs, to work in gold, silver, and bronze, in cutting stones for setting, and in carving wood, to work in every craft."

Other passages to consider are: Exodus 25:10-27:19; 28:2-43; 30:1-10; 39:1-43; Leviticus 8:6-9; 2 Chronicles 5:12-14; 7:6; 9:11; Psalm 33:1-3; Hebrews 8:5; 9:23, 24; Rev. 5:7,8. These passages speak of music, liturgy, vestments, craftsmanship, incense and beauty related to worship.

The Meaning and Symbols of Holy Eucharist

Therefore, these forms of worship are not medieval novelties as some of us have been taught, but preceded Christianity, and were the forms incorporated by the Early Church.

It may be argued that Jesus eradicated incense, vestments, liturgies, and the like, when he established the New Covenant. But I invite the reader to consider Jesus' statement in Matthew 5:17, "Do not think that I have come to abolish the Law or the Prophets: I have come to fulfill them." Jesus is speaking primarily, I believe, of his purpose in fulfilling the sacrificial system for the sake of atonement – of paying the full price for sin in a way that the blood of bulls and goats cannot for the salvation of humanity [see Hebrews 10:1-14]. Even so, he does not simply dismiss the rest of the Law and the Prophets, but goes on to say in verse 18, "For truly, I say to you, until heaven and earth pass away, not an iota, not a dot will pass away from the Law until it is accomplished."

Certainly, his atonement has been accomplished through his self-offering as the Passover Lamb on Good Friday and resurrection on Easter. But God's people continue to relate to God based on the standards and commandments that He laid out in the Old Covenant and those that Jesus enriched and fulfilled in the New. While we are no longer obligated to follow the sacrificial law – especially in its insufficient form (that which predates Jesus), we are blessed to follow the moral form (that which is re-constituted in Christ and reflects the heart of God). In this way, we understand that Baptism is of a similar character to that of Circumcision, and transcends it. [Colossians 2:11,12] Holy Eucharist

The Meaning and Symbols of Holy Eucharist

declares the truths presented in the Passover, and yet goes far beyond what even the Passover could accomplish and proclaim. [1 Corinthians 5:7,8] The enrichment of the Old Covenant signs is why the author to the Hebrews declares the "law is only a shadow of the good things that are coming – not the realities themselves." [Hebrews 10:1] Christian worship ought to teach and demonstrate these greater realities in a corresponding manner. [Compare Exodus 12:24-27; Deuteronomy 6:4-9, 20]

The symbols, colors and images used in liturgical worship have a didactic quality to them. They are intended to communicate something more than abstract beauty. Neither are the symbols random, but they are presented in an orderly way through the Church Year. The Church Year unfolds as a grand drama to portray the full Salvation story. The seasons are like the scenes of an opera. When the curtain falls and rises again, the scene changes but it is part of the same drama moving toward the final act.

The following seasons are listed in chronological order with their predominant color and the Gospel lessons that define the season, Matthew being Year A, Mark being Year B, and Luke being Year C. This is generally the case, however some feast days retain the same lessons every year. The accompanying descriptions are intended to be both descriptive and devotional. The reader should be advised that traditions for certain seasons, especially Lent, vary widely from region to region and church to church. I have presented here what is fairly common in my experience as both parishioner and priest, but do not be surprised if your church celebrates the festivals differently.

The Meaning and Symbols of Holy Eucharist

Advent

(Purple/Violet/Dark Blue*)

Matthew 24:37-44; Mark 13:24-37; Luke 21:25-31

The Church year begins with the first Sunday in Advent, in November. *Advent* is from a Latin word, which means *to come* and reminds us to prepare for Jesus' birth, and His Second Coming. It is marked by the color purple, Advent wreaths and candles, Advent hymns (O come, O come, Emmanuel), and a somber expectant atmosphere. While not as penitential as Lent (see below), Advent also calls the worshippers to self-reflection, preparation, and repentance. John the Baptist's call to "Prepare the way of the Lord" dominates the lessons.

*Note: some traditions make a distinction in colors between the color displayed in Advent and that used in Lent.

The Meaning and Symbols of Holy Eucharist

Christmas

or *Feast of the Holy Nativity*

(White/Gold*)

Luke 2:1-20

Christmas follows Advent, beginning with the Feast of the Holy Nativity on Christmas Eve (Not the day after Thanksgiving!). The word "Christmas" tells us this. *Christmas* is a contraction of *Christ's Mass*, which is the celebration of the Eucharist at Christ's nativity. (*Mass* is an Old English word for *festival* or *feast,* derived from the Latin word *missa* for *dismissal.)* Special celebrations in the Church year are called Feast Days. These feast days assume that *the* Feast is the Lord's Supper (Holy Eucharist). So, the word *Christmas* literally means *Christ's Eucharist.* Christmas is marked by the color white (and gold), with poinsettias, greenery, and the lit Christmas candle. The Christmas season ends with Epiphany on January 6th, hence the twelve days of Christmas. During the twelve days of Christmas comes the solemn remembrance of the slaughter of the Holy Innocents on December 28th, which commemorates the ruthless massacre of the children of Bethlehem (Matthew 2:16). January 1st is remembered as the Feast of the Holy Name (Luke 2:21). The eighth day after a Jewish boy was born, he would be named and circumcised.

For vestments and paraments, gold is not a color like yellow, it is cloth-of-gold, which may be used in place of white for major feasts. Gold is representative of God's glory.

The Meaning and Symbols of Holy Eucharist

Epiphany

or *The Manifestation of Christ*

(White)

Matthew 2:1-12

Epiphany, like Christmas, is a feast day that is locked to a specific date – in this case January 6th. Epiphany celebrates the visit of the Magi and the gifts given to Jesus. In fact, for some Christians, gifts are given on each of the twelve days of Christmas, or at the end of the twelve days (Epiphany) rather than on Christmas day. This tradition preserves the celebration of Christ's incarnation and birth on the feast of the Holy Nativity, and the attribution of gift giving as complementing that of the Magi on Epiphany. The Sundays following Epiphany commemorate other events in Jesus' life where his divinity is made manifest, such as Jesus' baptism in the river Jordan and the miracle at the Marriage Feast in Cana. The days following the Feast of the Epiphany (or, the Presentation in the UK) are part of Ordinary Time and marked by the color green, as are the days following Pentecost (see Ordinary Time below). Some traditions mark the end of the Epiphany Season with the Feast of the Presentation (or Candlemas) on February $2^{nd.}$ The Presentation marks the fortieth day after Jesus' birth, when Mary was presented for her purification and Jesus to be redeemed as the first-born son, according to the Law.

Lent

(Purple/Violet)

Matthew 6:1-6, 16-21

Lent is a season of forty days that begins with Ash Wednesday and ends with lighting the First Fire and the Paschal Candle at the Easter Vigil (more on that later). During the week of the Last Sunday after Epiphany, comes a popular feasting day called Shrove Tuesday. In the English tradition pancake suppers are a favorite offering for Shrove Tuesday. Outside of Anglicanism, *Shrove Tuesday* is better known as *Fat Tuesday* or *Mardi Gras*. It is a day of feasting, because it marks the last day to eat rich foods – to clean out the cupboards before Lent begins on Ash Wednesday, which is a day of fasting. There are two mandatory fasts in Lent: Ash Wednesday and Good Friday. It should be noted that exceptions are made for the elderly, those who are ill and children.

Unfortunately, some people view Mardi Gras (like Saint Patrick's Day) as a license to get drunk and take their clothes off. (One wonders if they will enter the solemnity of Lent with equal enthusiasm.) Ironically, the purpose of Lent, which is well expressed in the lessons and pleadings of Ash Wednesday, is aimed to help us recognize how destructive sin is; that we are in desperate need of a Savior. "for all have sinned and fall short of the glory of God" as Saint Paul revealed [Romans 3.23].

The Meaning and Symbols of Holy Eucharist

Ash Wednesday uses language and imagery that sound hauntingly similar to the Prayer Book's graveside service: "dust to dust, and ashes to ashes." As the black ashes are imposed on the penitent's forehead in the sign of the cross, she hears, "Remember O woman thou art dust, and to dust thou shalt return."

Ashes are difficult to wash off; try it sometime.

The debauchery of a hedonistic Mardi Gras comes with a horrific price: there must be a reckoning of accounts. Sin is not undone by a dose of Tylenol, nor by a visit to an abortion clinic. There is no justice in that. Imagine a rapist offering a candy bar to his victim and flippantly saying "Sorry" in the process. Who would account that as adequate? And yet we expect much more of God, if we expect anything at all. We expect Him to be pleased with our cavalier "sorries" as if we are exempt from the same justice that we expect for others. Others must pay, but surely God isn't bothered by what I do. [See 2 Samuel chapters 11 and 12]

The forty days of Lent invite us to sincerely examine our relationship with God, to urge us out of rationalization and self-justification, toward repentance and reconciliation.

The atmosphere of Lent changes in a number ways: Crosses are veiled in purple; God's people are called to fast; alleluias, glorias and flowers are omitted from the Liturgies. In short, we are exposed to consider life without the love and mercy of Christ. We are also invited to take a pilgrimage to the Holy Land by means of walking the

The Meaning and Symbols of Holy Eucharist

Stations of the Cross where Jesus' Passion is remembered. In the Middle Ages Christians would make a pilgrimage to Jerusalem for Holy Week. Over time, a tradition of setting up images of the Stations at one's local parish became popular for those who could not go to Jerusalem, making it possible for everyone to make a pilgrimage.

+

For if after renouncing Satan and associating thyself with Christ, thou fall under their influence, thou shalt find the tyrant more bitter; perchance, because he treated thee of old as his own, and relieved thee from his hard bondage, but has now been greatly exasperated by thee; so thou wilt be bereaved of Christ, and have experience of the other.

Saint Cyril of Jerusalem – *Catechetical Lectures*

The Meaning and Symbols of Holy Eucharist

Passion Week
(Red/Purple/White/Black)

The traditions, liturgies and colors of Passion Week vary depending on the local tradition and practices of a parish. Parishes that follow an Anglo-Catholic tradition may produce a more liturgically complex observance of Holy Week. Whatever tradition you observe, the drama is palpable. While the Stations of the Cross may be traversed in 30 – 40 minutes, the Passion of Christ is remembered in real time during Passion Week.

Palm Sunday – *The Triumphal Entry*
(Red)

Matthew 26:36 – 27:66; Mark 14:32 – 15:47; Luke 22:39 – 23:56

On Palm Sunday we remember Jesus' entrance into Jerusalem the week of His Passion. The Liturgy of the Palms begins outside with the blessing of the palms, which are distributed to the gathered crowd. A brief liturgy is used with Matthew 21:1-11 (A); Mark 11-11a (B) or Luke 19:29-40 (C) read to set the stage, reminding us of Jesus sending the disciples out to fetch a donkey. A longer than usual procession begins outside with palms waved, bells rung and shouts given, followed by the hymn "All glory laud and honor" Jesus is hailed the King of the Jews with "Hosannas!" From all appearances, this will be a grand celebration. However, the joy is soon overturned as we come face-to-face with the fickle affections of the crowds,

The Meaning and Symbols of Holy Eucharist

while the Gospel narrative recounts the coming arrest and crucifixion.

Some churches will provide the Gospel narrative as a drama, with different people reading the various parts. Smaller congregations may just divide the readings between the part of Jesus, the narrator and the crowd, which is read by the congregation. In whatever form the Gospel is presented, the contrast between the joy of the people as Jesus enters Jerusalem and those days later who call for his crucifixion is striking. The solemnity is emphasized by the congregation standing at the mention of "Golgotha" and bowing/kneeling in silence when Jesus gives up his spirit.

Maundy Thursday

(White)

John 13:1-15; Luke 22:14-30

During the evening on Maundy Thursday we remember the Last Supper, Jesus washing the feet of the disciples, and the New Commandment that He presented to the disciples that they must love one another, and the vigil at the Garden of Gethsemane.

As with Palm Sunday, Maundy Thursday presents a liturgy filled with anticipation and tension. The liturgy presents Jesus' love for His disciples through a ceremony of foot washing, which is usually offered by the Celebrant. As the

The Meaning and Symbols of Holy Eucharist

Celebrant represents Christ at the Altar, so he represents Him humbly at the footwashing, where members of the congregation are invited to come forward to have their feet washed.

Even though it is Lent, the altar and clergy are vested in white, celebrating the Last Supper with the disciples, which is in reality the First Supper for the Church. However, the celebration soon turns to anxiety as Jesus leaves the supper table and leads His disciples to Gethsemane. After the congregation has received Holy Communion, one of the clergy solemnly carries the Blessed Sacrament to the Garden of Repose. The Garden of Repose is a place set aside with candles and flowers and kneelers (or chairs) where people may pray and keep the vigil. As the Bread of Life is removed from the Sanctuary, other servers extinguish the candles. The aumbry/tabernacle is noticeably empty, while the servers strip the altar of everything that is bright, colorful and valuable. After the Stripping of the Altar, the emptiness and silence are arresting. The drama of the arrest is not presented to us as we might expect. It is not presented at all. The Liturgy ends in silence and darkness while the people quietly leave to take their vigil in the Garden of Repose.

The trajectory of the Maundy Thursday liturgy will be resumed with the Good Friday Liturgy of the following day.

Note: "Maundy" comes from the Latin term mandatum for "commandment". [See John 13:34]

The Meaning and Symbols of Holy Eucharist

Good Friday

(Black/Purple)

John 18:1 – 19:37

Why is Good Friday "good"? It is good because Jesus bore the sin of all humanity, it being nailed to the cross. Jesus received the condemnation due to sinners and reconciled us to the Father. The wooden cross is the counterpoint to the Tree of the Knowledge of Good and Evil. Adam and Eve invited sin and the reign of the Evil One into the world by yielding to that tree's temptation. Jesus reversed the Fall by nailing sin to the hard wood of the cross. Even in the midst of Jesus' suffering and death, we recognize that it was good for us. The Good Friday Liturgy is a service where the worshippers lament their sins and offer their gratitude to Jesus for His gracious sacrifice for us. This gratitude is expressed in the Good Friday Liturgy by the presentation of a Crucifix or rude cross, held by acolytes in a place where the worshippers can come and kneel before the cross in devotion and thanksgiving. Some will express their affection following one of the oldest traditions in Christendom: kissing the foot of the cross/crucifix. This in no way is intended as idol worship, but is a physical way to give thanksgiving to Jesus for his sacrifice.

Good Friday remembrances and walking the Stations of the Cross are among the most ancient Christian liturgies. The earliest Christians made pilgrimages to Jerusalem to walk in the footsteps of Jesus following his arrest and ascent to Golgotha. A riveting account of this is presented in the

The Meaning and Symbols of Holy Eucharist

journals of the Abbess Egeria of her pilgrimage to Jerusalem in the late the fourth century:

"Then a chair is placed for the bishop in Golgotha behind the Cross, which is now standing; the bishop duly takes his seat in the chair, and a table covered with a linen cloth is placed before him; the deacons stand round the table, and a silver-gilt casket is brought in which is the holy wood of the Cross. The casket is opened and (the wood) is taken out, and both the wood of the Cross and the title [Pilate's inscription - Matthew 27:37] are placed upon the table. Now, when it has been put upon the table, the bishop, as he sits, holds the extremities of the sacred wood firmly in his hands, while the deacons who stand around guard it. It is guarded thus because the custom is that the people, both faithful and catechumens, come one by one and, bowing down at the table, kiss the sacred wood and pass through. And because, I know not when, some one is said to have bitten off and stolen a portion of the sacred wood, it is thus guarded by the deacons who stand around, lest any one approaching should venture to do so again. And as all the people pass by one by one, all bowing themselves, they touch the Cross and the title, first with their foreheads and then with their eyes; then they kiss the Cross and pass through, but none lays his hand upon it to touch it."

[Excerpt from *The Pilgrimage of Etheria* (aka Egeria), *Good Friday.-- Service at Daybreak.* by Egeria, Abbess and Pilgrim to Jerusalem (late 4th century):

http://www.ccel.org/m/mcclure/etheria/etheria.htm]

The Meaning and Symbols of Holy Eucharist

Local traditions vary greatly regarding the remembrances of Good Friday in our day. The Stations of the Cross (or Way of the Cross) are commonly observed. Traditionally, the Eucharist is not celebrated on this day, to emphasize Jesus' death and temporary separation from his disciples. However, many churches will offer Communion from the Reserved Sacrament (also called "the Pre-Sanctifed") following the Veneration of the Cross.

Holy Saturday

(Red)

Matthew 27:57-66; John 19:38-42

Holy Saturday commemorates Christ's descent to Hades, breaking down the gates of death and preaching the Good News to the spirits in prison. [See 1 Peter 3:19; Luke 4:18] It is worth noting here the difference between Hades and Hell. The King James Version of the Holy Scriptures has confused this distinction by translating the Greek word *hades*, as *hell*. However, *hades* is the equivalent to the Old Testament Hebrew term, *sheol*, both of which refer to the place of the dead. In the New Testament the place of final judgment for the damned is *gehenna*, which is appropriately translated as *hell*. [Compare Luke 16:19-31 (*hades*) and Mark 9:38-48 (*hell*). The New American Standard Bible, for example, is careful to retain this distinction]

The Meaning and Symbols of Holy Eucharist

What did you see? Water, certainly, but not water alone; you saw the deacons ministering there, and the bishop asking questions and hallowing. First of all, the Apostle taught you that those things are not to be considered "which we see, but the things which are not seen, for the things which are seen are temporal, but the things which are not seen are eternal."

Saint Ambrose– *The Sacred Mysteries*

The Meaning and Symbols of Holy Eucharist

Easter

The Resurrection of our Lord Jesus Christ,

(White/Gold)

Matthew 28:1-10; Mark 16:1-8; Luke 24:1-10

In the Early Church, the "sunrise service" was not the first worship service of Easter, it was the conclusion of a Liturgy and worship that had begun Saturday evening and continued through the night with the Biblical stories of God's salvation, the baptism of catechumens (those being prepared for baptism), and concluding with the celebration of Holy Eucharist timed to correspond to the sunrise. Prior to their baptism, the catechumens were not allowed to observe the celebration of the Eucharist, but were ushered off to an extensive catechism (instruction). The catechumens received catechism for one or two years, making their confessions during Lent in preparation for their baptism during the Great Vigil of Easter. Because of the great risk of suffering and martyrdom for the Faith, it was deemed essential that catechumens be very certain of their Faith, before making such a serious commitment.

The Easter Vigil is the "mother of all Liturgies." It creates the standard for the rest of the year and all other celebrations. It begins outside on Saturday night with the "First Fire" when a flint is used to ignite kindling in a basin. The fire is blessed while worshippers look on. The Paschal candle is marked with the nails of the cross and blessed. (This same Paschal candle will be lit and present

The Meaning and Symbols of Holy Eucharist

at the font for baptisms throughout the year.) The Paschal candle is lit from the first fire, and the deacon carries the paschal candle chanting the Exsultet, beginning with "the Light of Christ" as the worshippers respond "thanks be to God" while their candles are lit, and the procession of laity and clergy follow the Light of Christ into the dark church. Light flows into the church as the deacon's voice reverberates throughout. The deacon places the Paschal candle into the stand near the altar and continues the Exsultet facing the candle, "All you who stand near this marvelous and holy flame, pray with me to God the Almighty for the grace to sing the worthy praise of this great light; through Jesus Christ his Son our Lord . . ."

After the Exsultet, all of the lights in the church are lit and the people are seated to listen to the extensive readings of God's salvation beginning with Genesis and the story of creation. Bible lessons, prayers, psalms and canticles alternate throughout the evening, building the story of God's deliverance of his people. The Vigil lessons are followed by baptisms and/or the renewal of baptismal vows.

One tradition embeds the baptism within the Litany of the Saints, where the people and clergy walk out of the church still holding their candles in procession behind the Thurifer (an acolyte carrying a censer smoking with incense), Crucifer (the one holding the cross), acolytes with candles, and the cantor singing the Litany. The procession beckons the prayers of the saints and brings the Light of Christ back out to the world banishing the darkness in preparation for the baptism of the catechumens (or candidates), whose

The Meaning and Symbols of Holy Eucharist

spiritual darkness will be banished by the light of Christ through Holy Baptism. The worshippers process around the church (or other route) returning to the front doors of the church where the baptismal font, and holy oil is prepared.

The baptismal candidates gather near the font and celebrant with their backs to the church facing the world. The celebrant blesses the water, dipping the Paschal candle in three times, mindful of Jesus' own baptism in the Jordan where he hallowed the waters of the world for all future baptisms. The candidates renounce Satan, the world, and sinful desires [BCP 302]. The celebrant prays a prayer of exorcism over the candidates and then has them turn to face the church, their backs to the world as he asks, "Do you turn to Christ and accept him as your Savior?" The candidates then proclaim Christ as their Savior, in whom they put their whole trust, and promise to follow and obey as Lord. There is nothing half-hearted or shallow in this Liturgy! The candidates are baptized in the name of the Father, and the Son, and the Holy Spirit. They receive candles bearing both their names and the Light of Christ, which proclaims their adoption into the family of God, the Church. Now the Body marches triumphantly back into the church with no outsiders (ideally) concluding the Litany of the Saints. Now everyone gathered is included in the Supper of the Lamb – the newly baptized able to receive Holy Communion for the first time in their new skin.

Now gathered as one body around the altar, all sing the Gloria - "Glory to God in the Highest, and peace to his people on earth!" Bells ring out loudly through the assembly as the Gloria is sung with exuberance. There is much to celebrate: Lent is over! Those who were lost are saved! Christ is risen from the grave! Alleluia! Alleluia! Christ is risen indeed!

After the Gloria, the people sit for the lessons of the Eucharist, which are simple and brief compared to the earlier Vigil lessons. Romans 6:3-11 is read and the Gospel of Matthew 28:1-10 is read by the deacon. Very likely no one will offer a homily because the lessons and the Liturgy are so powerful on their own that a homily hardly seems necessary. At this point in the Liturgy, the people may already have been worshipping for two or three hours, and it is probably nearing midnight, and yet there is so much joy and expectation for the celebration of the Eucharist that a holy energy fills the sanctuary.

Imagine the attitude of those in the Early Church who spent two years preparing for this moment where they were finally received into the Church and able to receive the Holy Mysteries. This is why the Great Vigil of Easter is the "mother of all Liturgies." In it is fulfilled the Great Commission and the Lord's establishment of the two primary sacraments: Holy Baptism and Holy Eucharist. The two come together bathed in the Light of Christ breaking through a world lost in darkness. As noted above, all that was described here for an evening service reaching its climax at midnight (Easter Sunday), the Early church observed throughout the night finding its climatic realization with the celebration of Holy Eucharist as the sun rose, along with the rising of the Son.

The Meaning and Symbols of Holy Eucharist

This is the message we have heard from him and proclaim to you, that God is light, and in him is no darkness at all. If we say we have fellowship with him while we walk in darkness, we lie and do not practice the truth. But if we walk in the light, as he is in the light, we have fellowship with one another, and the blood of Jesus his Son cleanses us from all sin. 1 John 1:5-7 [ESV]

Ascension Day

(White)

Luke 24:49-53; Mark 16:9-15, 19-20

After the forty days of Lent leading into Easter, we find ourselves once again in a forty day period of time leading to Ascension Day. Have you noticed that there are a lot of Forties in Scripture? There are forty days and forty nights of rain for the flood of Noah; forty years wandering in the wilderness with Moses after escaping Egypt; Jesus fasted forty days in the wilderness; the disciples had forty days with Jesus between his resurrection and ascension.

Have you ever wondered what that must have been like? They had three years with Jesus not understanding his comments that he must suffer and die, and then be raised. They had lived under the tension of knowing that the Jewish leaders wanted to arrest Jesus, and so avoided Jerusalem much of the time.

The Meaning and Symbols of Holy Eucharist

Then the disciples find themselves in transition between the feasts of Passover and Pentecost, where Jesus, whom they saw crucified, appears to them periodically and unexpectedly, demonstrating that he is still a real human being. He passes through a door and then invites Thomas to touch him: he's real! He invites them to a fish barbeque on the beach: he's real! What is the significance of the forty days?

Forty days (or forty years) in Scripture seem to set apart a period of transition. During that transition God gives his people opportunities to wait on Him, to trust Him, and to encounter Him. Before Jesus ascended to the Father, he ensured that the disciples understood that he is still a real human being, that he kept all of his promises to them, and showed them that the messianic prophecies were fulfilled in him. This was to prepare them for the Holy Spirit's arrival at Pentecost.

And for this reason three seasons of the year prefigured the Savior Himself, so that He should fulfill the mysteries prophesied of Him. In the Passover season, so as to exhibit Himself as one destined to be sacrificed like a sheep, and to prove Himself the true Paschal lamb, even as the apostle says, "Even Christ," who is God, "our passover was sacrificed for us." And at Pentecost so as to presignify the kingdom of heaven as He Himself first ascended to heaven and brought man as a gift to God.

Saint Hippolytus – *Fragment, Section V*

The Meaning and Symbols of Holy Eucharist

Pentecost
(Red)

Acts 2:1-21; John 20:19-23; John 14:8-17

Pentecost refers to the fifty days between Passover and Pentecost. Ascension is always celebrated on the Thursday prior to Pentecost, which is forty days after Easter (Passover). Passover and Pentecost are Jewish celebrations that took on a new significance in Christianity.

Luke's Gospel was originally offered in two volumes. It is unfortunate that the Gospel of John separates them. Matthew, Mark and Luke follow a similar style of presenting the story of Christ. Therefore, they are referred to as the Synoptic Gospels. The accounts in the synoptics are short and pithy, moving the story along rapidly. John, however, provides long intimate narratives, which are designed to invites us into the relationship enjoyed by "the disciple whom Jesus loved" [John 13:23].

Luke's two-volume work presents the story of Jesus' life, and continues with the Acts of the Apostles. Luke is demonstrating a cause and effect: Jesus the Cause, the Church the effect. The hinge to these two works is Pentecost. Jesus promised that when he ascended into heaven, he would send the Comforter [John 14:16]. The birth of the Church, is the coming of the Holy Spirit at Pentecost: the Church becoming the Body of Christ, carrying out the Great Commission as his ambassadors [2 Corinthians 5:0]. This fits well with the Triune proclamation of the Nicene Creed. God, the Father predominates the Old Testament. Jesus, the Son is the center of the Gospels, and God the Holy Spirit is most prominent from the age of the Apostles (the Church), beginning at Pentecost and continuing into the present.

+

Open, then, your ears, inhale the good savour of eternal life which has been breathed upon you by the grace of the sacraments; which was signified to you by us, when, celebrating the mystery of the opening, we said, "Epphatha, which is, Be opened," that whosoever was coming in quest of peace might know what he was asked, and be bound to remember what he answered.

Saint Ambrose – *The Sacred Mysteries*

The Meaning and Symbols of Holy Eucharist

Ordinary Time
(Green)

Ordinary Time: the days between Epiphany and Lent, and between Trinity and Advent

The word "ordinary" is used in the Church in two unique ways:

(1) The bishop of a diocese is referred to as "the Ordinary", which is why his assistant is called "the Canon to the Ordinary". We have come to think of "ordinary" as meaning common, mundane or boring. But that is not the meaning in the Church. The diocesan bishop (or simply, *Diocesan*) is the Ordinary, because he is responsible for maintaining the faith, standards and structure of the Church within his cure and anywhere he might have influence. The Ordinary promotes order. The standard-bearing Ordinary is the one who *ordains ordinands*, using the *ordinal*. Those under Holy Orders being assistants in the mission to promote the orderly Faith of the Church. In this sense, *orderly* means the Ordinary ensures that what is practiced and taught to those under his pastoral care is the Faith that he received from the Apostles through Holy Scripture, and Apostolic Succession by the laying on of hands (Acts 6:6; 8:18; 1 Timothy 4:14; 5:22; 2 Timothy 1:6) Therefore, the bishop makes the Christian Faith *ordinary* (or normative) without dilution or enhancement. To be ordinary in this sense is to be unchanging, with respect to the Faith of the Church. This doesn't sound pleasant to modern ears where change – any kind of change – is

The Meaning and Symbols of Holy Eucharist

viewed more favorably than anything that is perceived as old-fashioned, stagnant, stale and inflexible.

(2) The days of the Church year are also ordered. Those days that are measured between the great festivals of the year are called "Ordinary Time." They fall between Epiphany-Presentation and Lent, and between Pentecost-Trinity and Advent. These days are marked by the color green, and the lessons primarily direct us toward discipleship, which is personal growth (Sanctification) and sharing the Good News of Jesus (Evangelism). The lessons during Ordinary Time do not relate to special seasons but to observing how God related to His people in the Old Testament, and especially to how Jesus taught His disciples and ministered to the people of Judea and environs. Ordinary Time invites us into the ordinary daily life of Jesus and His disciples during His ministry. Wherein Jesus brought life-giving order into the lives of people trapped by the chaotic darkness of the evil one. As the Word of God made flesh, Jesus became the real and living expression of God's revelation to humanity, which when received in faith brings peace (or order) into our lives.

Therefore, the Sundays after Pentecost are not the "Season *of* Pentecost" as some mistakenly call them. They are the Sundays *after* Pentecost, (or, the Sundays after Trinity) and they reach their culmination with Christ the King Sunday one week before Advent begins. If you are most familiar with the 1979 Book of Common Prayer Lectionary (US),

The Meaning and Symbols of Holy Eucharist

then you are accustomed to seeing something like the "7th Sunday after Pentecost" during Ordinary Time. The 1662 (UK) and 1928 Book of Common Prayer (US), along with the book of Common Worship (UK), count Ordinary Time *after* Trinity Sunday (the Sunday following Pentecost). Similarly, Ordinary Time following Epiphany is calculated after the Baptism of Christ in the US, and after the Presentation in the UK. The readings and collects during Ordinary Time are also referred to as "the Propers". You will find a more detailed introduction to the use of the propers on page 158 of the 1979 BCP, and examples of the proper collects begin on page 176 (Traditional) and page 228 (Contemporary). The corresponding lessons are given in the Lectionary at the end of the BCP beginning on page 896.

Ordinary Time tutors us to embrace the daily life of discipleship – that is, to follow Jesus through the common days as well as the great festivals. As bright and beautiful as Christmas and Easter are, our faith is to be expressed and celebrated in the common and ordinary moments of life as well.

The Meaning and Symbols of Holy Eucharist

Saints and Martyrs
(White and Red)

Matthew 5:1-12; Luke 6:20-36

Saints and martyrs never occupy center stage on Sundays, with one exception, when All Saints Day (November 1st) falls on a Sunday. Why is this? Because the Saints are all gathered together because of their faithfulness in honoring Christ. Their praises are not for one another but for Christ. Their examples are not to bring praise to themselves, but to Christ, while encouraging us to do the same. [Hebrews 12:1]

The word "martyr" is the Greek word for "witness". The martyrs are witnesses giving their testimony in the cosmic courtroom that Christ is the victorious Son of God. The days of the principalities and powers are numbered [Philippians 2:9-11].

Therefore, individual saints are only remembered on weekdays. The priest vests in red for those who were martyred, and in white for those who died of natural causes.

The Meaning and Symbols of Holy Eucharist

[Julian] met with a man who promised to predict these things, conducted him into one of the idol temples, introduced him within the shrine, and called upon the demons of deceit. On their appearing in their wonted aspect, terror compelled Julian to make the sign of the cross upon his brow. They no sooner saw the sign of the Lord's victory than they were reminded of their own rout, and forthwith fled away. On the magician becoming acquainted with the cause of their flight he blamed him; but Julian confessed his terror, and said that he wondered at the power of the cross, for that the demons could not endure to see its sign and ran away.

The Ecclesiastical History of Theodoret

CHAPTER THREE

Common Symbols

*Behold the Lamb of God
who takes away the sin of the world!*
John 1:29

There are numerous symbols used by Christians to signify certain truths of Christianity. Symbols are powerful as they have the potential to communicate very complex and profound truths with just a single image. Many find their origins in the beginning of Christianity. Here we will simply describe a few of the most common symbols.

Chi Rho

Chi and *Rho* are the first two letters of the Greek alphabet in the title *Christ*, which means *anointed one*. They are represented in English by the letters "XP". Often the letters are overlapped to form a symbol which represents Christ. XP (chi rho) then serves as both a symbol and an abbreviation for the name of Christ.

The Meaning and Symbols of Holy Eucharist

Chi rho is often abbreviated further to simply *Chi* as in "X-mas." However, this should never be pronounced e*cksmas*, as if Christ were removed from the name, since the "X" does not stand for the English "X" (ecks) but rather the Greek "X" (chi). Therefore, while written "X-mas", it is verbalized as "Christmas", which itself is an abbreviation of *Christ's Mass* – a reference to the celebration of the Eucharist on the Feast of the Holy Nativity.

The Meaning and Symbols of Holy Eucharist

Cross, Crucifix and Christus Rex

To have a body or not to have a body; that is the question.

Since the Reformation Movement, Christians have reignited the controversy over whether or not an image of Jesus breaks the first commandment. This was controversial even during the Early Church, but the Seventh Ecumenical Council, the Second Council of Nicea (787), determined that icons and images were an aid to prayer and worship if they were merely venerated but not worshipped themselves. However, many Christians are still uncomfortable with a representation of the body of Christ (corpus) included on a cross.

The Meaning and Symbols of Holy Eucharist

Therefore, some Christians only allow plain crosses hanging in and around their churches. Others have one of two bodies attached to the cross: a dead and bleeding body known as a Crucifix, or a robed and crowned body known as a Christus Rex. The Crucifix is presented to remind believers of Jesus' loving sacrifice, where he gave himself up for the sins of the world. [Acts 2.23; 2 Corinthians 5.21]

The Christus Rex, or Christ the King, is presented to remind believers of Jesus resurrected and ascended to the right hand of God, as King of Kings. [Romans 8.34; 1 Timothy 6.15; Revelation 19.16]

The Meaning and Symbols of Holy Eucharist

Fish and Sign of the Cross

This image may well be the oldest and best known of Christian symbols. As the story is told, the earliest Christians used the symbol like a secret handshake to identify one another during the early decades of Christian persecution. One person might approach another thinking that he might be a Christian and casually draw an arc in the dirt with his foot. If the other person responded in kind with an opposite arc to produce a simple image of a fish, the two could be assured that it was safe to have fellowship.

A similar tradition is told of the sign of the cross made when a person takes her right hand touching forehead, mid-section and shoulders. During the age of persecutions, this silent sign would be made when a worshipper entered a hidden church to show the gate-keeper deacons that she was a true believer, without exposing the sign to potential persecutors who might be behind her. Later, the sign of the cross became simply an expression of belief in Christ, and is used as a proclamation of honor for the Presence of Christ when someone genuflects before the Reserved Sacrament, or bows before a Crucifix or Christus Rex.

The Meaning and Symbols of Holy Eucharist

The Gospels and the Four Living Creatures

One of the most intriguing sets of symbols in the Church is one of which you may only catch a glimpse from time to time. You may see it on the ornate Gospel Book cover, or on the pulpit, or lectern. It is a set of four images: human, lion, ox and eagle.

Each figure is placed into one of the quadrants created by the image of the cross. These images are represented in the form of cherubim and are associated with the Gospel Book, and or the preaching of the Gospel. The four living creatures, (or cherubim) occur several times in the Bible and were eventually associated with the four Gospel writers.

The Four Living Creatures in Scripture

Ezekiel 1:10-14 *Their faces looked like this: Each of the four had the face of a man, and on the right side each had the face of a lion, and on the left the face of an ox; each also had the face of an eagle. Such were their faces. Their wings were spread out upward; each had two wings, one touching the wing of another creature on either side, and two wings covering its body. Each one went straight ahead. Wherever the spirit would go, they would go, without turning as they went. The appearance of the living creatures was like burning coals of fire or like torches. Fire moved back and forth among the creatures; it was bright, and lightning flashed out of it. The creatures sped back and forth like flashes of lightning.*

Revelation 4:6-8 *In the center, around the throne, were four living creatures, and they were covered with eyes, in front and in back. The first living creature was like a lion, the second was like an ox, the third had a face like a man, the fourth was like a flying eagle. Each of the four living creatures had six wings and was covered with eyes all around, even under his wings. Day and night they never stop saying:*

The Meaning and Symbols of Holy Eucharist

"Holy, holy, holy is the Lord God Almighty, who was, and is, and is to come."

Jewish tradition.
- Human: the highest of creatures (the creature made in the image of God)
- Lion: the king of wild beasts
- Ox: the chief of domestic beasts
- Eagle: the greatest of birds

Early Church tradition.

The Church fathers later attributed the following symbolism to the Gospels:

Matthew is represented by a human. [Intelligence]

Matthew begins with the human genealogy of Jesus:

> *The book of the genealogy of Jesus Christ, the son of David, the son of Abraham.* - Matthew 1.1

Mark is represented by a lion. [Nobility]

Mark begins with a voice crying in the wilderness:
> *As it is written in Isaiah the prophet, "Behold, I send my messenger before your face, who will prepare your way, the voice of one crying in the wilderness: 'Prepare the way of the Lord, make his paths straight,". . . and saying, "The time is fulfilled, and the kingdom of God is at hand; repent and believe in the gospel."* - Mark 1.2,3,15.

The Meaning and Symbols of Holy Eucharist

Luke is represented by an ox. [Strength]

Luke begins with the priestly office (sacrificial) of Zechariah:
> *In the days of Herod, king of Judea, there was a priest named Zechariah,a of the division of Abijah. And he had a wife from the daughters of Aaron, and her name was Elizabeth. And they were both righteous before God, walking blamelessly in all the commandments and statutes of the Lord. But they had no child, because Elizabeth was barren, and both were advanced in years.* - Luke 1.5-7

John is represented by an eagle. [Vision/Agility]

John's gospel begins with a dizzying vantage point:
> *In the beginning was the Word, and the Word was with God, and the Word was God.* - John 1.1

The Meaning and Symbols of Holy Eucharist

Icons

The icon above is the *Christ Pantocrator* (or, *Pantokrator*), one of the earliest and most well known icons, the oldest dating back to the sixth century in the monastery of Saint Catherine in the Sinai desert. "Pantokrator" is Greek for "All Powerful". The image is meant to convey the presence of Christ among us, as does the name Immanuel – *God with us*. [Isaiah 7.14; Matthew 1.23]. Icons have had a controversial history in the Church due to the understandable concern not to violate the Commandment.:

The Meaning and Symbols of Holy Eucharist

"Thou shalt not make unto thee any graven image, or any likeness of any thing that is in heaven above, or that is in the earth beneath . . ." Exodus 20.4a (KJV).

Icons came into common use in the Fifth century. Their use in the Greek Church became controversial in the Eighth and Ninth centuries. Historians refer to this as the Iconoclastic (*image-breaking*) Controversy. The Byzantine Emperor Leo III, saw them as an impediment to the conversion of Jews and Muslims, and outlawed their use by edict in 726, demanding they be destroyed. That edict was supported at the Synod of Hieria in 753. The Second Council of Nicea overturned the iconalcastic regulations in 787. Even so, the controversy was one of the factors that led to the Great Schism between the Western Church and the Eastern Church.

Anglicans relate to icons in much the same way they do to the practice of so-called prayers to the Saints: pragmatically. Have you ever tried to pray but found your mind kept wandering off to things you ought to do, or situations that you were worried about? Looking at an icon of Christ while praying can help you to stay focused in your prayers, much the same way that using a liturgy helps us not to be distracted. Furthermore, icons of the Saints remind us of the Church Triumphant that continues to pray for the Church Militant. [See Hebrews 12:1,2, and Revelation 6:9-11] While Anglicans believe in the ongoing prayers of the Saints, we don't pray *to* them but ask them to pray *for* us, as we might ask any Christian friend. Likewise, icons are not used as objects of worship, but as instruments for prayer.

IHS

IHS was not originally an acronym for the phrase "In His Service" as it is often used now to close correspondence. Nor was it first the sign for *In hoc signo vinces*, which stands for "In this sign conquer" traditionally attributed to the General Constantine who battled his way to become the first emperor of the Roman Empire to lead under a Christian ensign.

Its earliest use was to represent the first three letters of Jesus' name. In Greek the "J" is rendered with an "i", the "e" with an "h" and the "s" with an "s" - well one out of three is better than nothing! In Greek, the "j" is actually an iota (i), which is pronounced like our "y". This is clearer in some modern New Testament translations where the name

The Meaning and Symbols of Holy Eucharist

of Jesus is written as *Yeshua*, which is the same name as *Joshua*. No matter how you spell it, they all mean "Jehovah is salvation."

As with the XP (chi rho), the letters are often stacked on top of one another to make a unique symbol for the name of Jesus.

INRI

I.N.R.I are initials for the phrase placed above Jesus head on the cross. They stand for *Jesus of Nazareth; King of the Jews*. In Latin it was written *Iesus Nazarenus; Rex Iudaeorum.*

Jerusalem Cross

The Jerusalem cross is similar in design and significance to that of the cherubim engraved onto the Gospel Book. However, rather than living creatures in each quadrant, there are simple crosses. This signifies the proclamation of the gospel from Jerusalem to all corners of the world. It is also a cross commonly worn by those who have made a pilgrimage to Jerusalem.

The Meaning and Symbols of Holy Eucharist

Lamb of God (*Agnus Dei*)

The *Lamb of God* refers to Jesus as the Passover Lamb who takes away the sins of the world. *Agnus Dei* is the Latin phrase for *Lamb of God*. This symbol is portrayed as a lamb with a nimbus (halo) around its head; usually standing, but sometimes reclining, and generally with a wound in its side and a banner held beside it.

The Meaning and Symbols of Holy Eucharist

The Agnus Dei symbol is a visual rehearsal of the numerous passages, particularly in Revelation that describe the victorious Lamb of God, the nimbus symbolizing His holiness, the wound His crucifixion, and the banner His victory for the Church.

And they sang a new song, saying, "Worthy are you to take the scroll and to open its seals, for you were slain, and by your blood you ransomed people for God from every tribe and language and people and nation, and you have made them a kingdom and priests to our God, and they shall reign on the earth." Then I looked, and I heard around the throne and the living creatures and the elders the voice of many angels, numbering myriads of myriads and thousands of thousands, saying with a loud voice, "Worthy is the Lamb who was slain, to receive power and wealth and wisdom and might and honor and glory and blessing!" -- Revelation 5.9-12

Red Door

In a church with a traditional architectural layout, you will likely see it painted with a red door. The red door signifies that people enter into the Church through the blood of Christ. The symbolism of this is profound and carries through our entire progress into and within the Church. So that our physical entrance into a church building mirrors our entrance into the Church (or Body) of Christ and then continues our journey with the process of sanctification within the life of the Church, and the life of Christ. Correspondingly, you are likely to notice a font in the entry way (narthex) where baptisms are celebrated. The red door and the baptismal font are linked symbols marking the invitation made by the Apostle Peter on Pentecost:

Repent and be baptized everyone of you in the name of Jesus Christ for the forgiveness of your sins, and you will receive the gift of the Holy Spirit. For the promise is for you and your children and for all who are far off, everyone whom the Lord our God calls to himself. [Acts 2:38, 39 ESV]

The blood of Christ pays the penalty for our sins, providing the opportunity to repent and be baptized through both water and the Holy Spirit, allowing us to enter into a never-ending life of grace with God. That process is often described as *conversion* and the mercy given over our repentance is referred to as *justification* – that is, being made just or righteous before God through the merits of Christ. What follows justification then is the process of sanctification, which is the life-long process of drawing nearer to God. This is also referred to as "discipleship." So you may recognize here that the red door and font are both symbolic and real, as they point to, and offer the ground under which, we enter into the Church; the Life of Christ.

It is important at this point to notice the distinction between "church" and "Church." The *church* is as inferior to the *Church*, as are my child's toys in comparison to my love for my child. The church as a building is merely a building. The Church spoken of in Scripture and by the Church Fathers is the Living Body of Christ and the people

The Meaning and Symbols of Holy Eucharist

He has adopted and made into a transcendent family. The two should not be confused, even though the inferior physical structure points to the superior spiritual reality. In other words the beauty of stained glass windows and vestments is not to be taken at face value as merely the work of talented artisans, it is to be understood as pointing to a greater life-giving reality. For example, while stained glass windows provide beautiful light, their purpose is to point to the fact that worship transcends space, time and even death; that the patriarchs, saints and heavenly hosts are joining with us (or, we with them) in the everlasting worship of God! [See Hebrews 12:1 and Revelation 5:6-14]

Our entrance begins at the red door and font (justification) and then invites us into the Ark (sanctification), commonly described as the *Nave,* where hearing Holy Scripture and worship is normative. The Church is compared to Noah's Ark, as that which conveys us to salvation, in reflection of Saint Peter's observation:

. . . when God's patience waited in the days of Noah, while the ark was being prepared, in which a few, that is eight persons, were brought safely through water. Baptism, which corresponds to this, now saves you . . . [1 Peter 3:20b, 21a, ESV]

The nave is that portion of the church where the family gathers and enters into the routine life of the Church. It is the holy space between the narthex (entryway) and the sanctuary, where the altar sits. Ideally, the nave is the place where we do as a family, what we also practice as individuals: we abide in Christ. We serve, study, pray and worship, which is the life of sanctification. It is a life dedicated to service of Christ and our fellow man. This is

The Meaning and Symbols of Holy Eucharist

why many liturgies begin with what is called the Summary of the Law:

The first commandment is this: You shall love the Lord your God with all your heart, and with all your soul, and with all your mind, and with all your strength; and the second is like it: you shall love your neighbor as your self. There is no other commandment greater than these. [Mark 12:30, 31]

Justification is followed by sanctification, which is followed by ascension. This bring us to the third portion of our life in the Church. As baptized, faithful Christians who have been adopted and made heirs of the Kingdom of Heaven [Galatians 3:23 – 4:7], we have the ongoing invitation and full access to the very throne room of God the Father [Matthew 27:50-54]. The throne room of God was known to the Israelites as the Mercy Seat, which was within the Holy of Holies – the inner most sanctuary – in the Temple. This provided them with the security of experiencing the real presence of God in their midst. It certainly did not mean that God was not present anywhere else but it gave human beings, who understand things spatially and with their senses, a place in space and time to relate to God. Later, of course, God turned from being encased in a building, to being enfleshed in a person – His Son.

As, the people of Israel would make their pilgrimage up to Zion singing the Songs of Ascent, to make their sacrifices (worship), so now the people of Christ ascend to the altar to offer their sacrifices of praise and thanksgiving. The ascent from the nave to the altar equates to walking from the inner courtyard of the temple into the Holy of Holies, to bathe in the Presence of the Glory of God and receive His righteousness. The Celebrant wears the chasuble to declare to our eye that the Glory of God (the Shekinah) has descended upon us and upon the Gifts on the altar.

Whereas only the High Priest could enter into the Holy of Holies on the Day of Atonement, now through the blood of Christ, all Christians are priests [1 Peter 2:5], and all are invited into the Holy Presence. In His Presence we celebrate the victory of Christ over sin and death; the victory of our redemption, and most especially our union with God through the love of Christ. That love is offered to us in Christ's Body and Blood given to us by the eternally effectual Word of Christ: "Do this in remembrance of me." *Eucharist* means *thanksgiving*!

So from the moment we enter the doors of the church we are enacting (not pretending) the life of Faith: conversion, discipleship and victory. We begin our ascent at the red doors and continue up into the arms of Jesus at the altar. If we recognize this, then every movement from our entrance to the church draws closer to Jesus, and reinforces the essential value to exercise that in our lives throughout the week. Jesus does not only call us to life of discipleship and sanctification on Sunday within the church building, but to practice that as the template for our lives everyday, bringing the Church with us everywhere we go, modeling conversion, discipleship and victory.

Having read this, take a moment now to meditate on Psalm 23, noting how the Good Shepherd equips his sheep and then leads them through the valley of the shadow of death up to the banquet table.

The Meaning and Symbols of Holy Eucharist

Psalm 23

King James Version

1 The Lord is my shepherd; I shall not want.

2 He maketh me to lie down in green pastures: he leadeth me beside the still waters.

3 He restoreth my soul: he leadeth me in the paths of righteousness for his name's sake.

4 Yea, though I walk through the valley of the shadow of death, I will fear no evil: for thou art with me; thy rod and thy staff they comfort me.

5 Thou preparest a table before me in the presence of mine enemies: thou anointest my head with oil; my cup runneth over.

6 Surely goodness and mercy shall follow me all the days of my life: and I will dwell in the house of the Lord for ever.

CHAPTER FOUR

Introduction to Holy Eucharist

Perhaps you will say, "I see something else, how is it that you assert that I receive the Body of Christ?" And this is the point which remains for us to prove. And what evidence shall we make use of? Let us prove that this is not what nature made, but what the blessing consecrated, and the power of blessing is greater than that of nature, because by blessing nature itself is changed.

Saint Ambrose – *The Sacred Mysteries*

Scriptural and Historical Background

Jesus commanded his followers to participate in two supernatural activities: Holy Baptism [Matthew 28:18-20], and Holy Eucharist [Luke 22:19; 1 Corinthians 11:24]. These are sometimes referred to as the Dominical Sacraments, to denote their superiority over the other sacraments (confirmation, reconciliation of a penitent, holy matrimony, ordination, and unction).

The Meaning and Symbols of Holy Eucharist

The Holy Eucharist is also known as *Holy Communion* and *The Liturgy*. In the New Testament, it is described as the *Lord's Supper*.

The celebration of the Lord's Supper originates with the Passover meal that Jesus offered to his disciples the night before he was arrested. [Matthew 26:17-29; Mark 14:12-25; Luke 22:7-20; John 13:1f] As Jews, the disciples were accustomed to observing the annual Passover meal, where they remembered the liberation of Israel from slavery in Egypt. [Exodus 12:1-42] This event and the interlaced imagery provide the prophetic backdrop for Jesus' celebration with his disciples. The original Passover was a terrifying event where the Israelites hid in their homes waiting for the death angel to *pass over* them. Following the directions that Moses received from God, the Jews prepared and consumed a flawless lamb, and smeared the lamb's blood over the top and sides of their door frames on the night that the death angel came to slaughter all of the firstborn males whose doorposts were not covered by the blood of the lamb [Exodus 12:3]. The lamb and the vertical and horizontal doorposts look forward to the vertical and horizontal beams of the cross on which the Lamb of God hung bleeding in order to deliver His people from the death angel.

Saint Paul gave instructions and emphasized the importance of observing the Lord's Supper with a holy attitude in his first letter to the Corinthian church [1 Corinthians 11:17-34]. Likewise, the second and third generation leaders known as the Early Church Fathers provided both teaching and liturgies for the celebration of

The Meaning and Symbols of Holy Eucharist

the Eucharist. [See Hippolytus, The Didache, and St. Ignatius, among others.]

The Book of Common Prayer in English was introduced by Archbishop Thomas Cranmer, during the reign of King Henry the VIII in 1549. Archbishop Cranmer's goal was to provide a liturgy in the common tongue that would enable the general populace to worship in their own language. Archbishop Cranmer also made English Bibles and homilies available. Since then, the 1662 Book of Common Prayer has become the standard prayer book throughout the Anglican Communion. The Church of England has also authorized the 2000 edition of the Book of Common Worship, which uses contemporary English.

After the Declaration of Independence and the war with Britain, Anglicans in the newly formed United States dropped the name *Anglican,* with all of its loyalist implications, and formed the Protestant Episcopal Church in 1789. The Episcopal Church also produced the first American Book of Common Prayer in 1789, which is very similar to the later 1928 Book of Common Prayer that remained as the American standard until 1979. In the 1960s Roman Catholics and Episcopalians were very interested in Liturgical Renewal and the development of liturgies that would be more appealing to modern ears. Correspondingly, there was an interest in ecumenism, and the use of ancient liturgies. Therefore the 1979 Book of Common Prayer incorporates elements of both Eastern and Western Rites, as well as many ancient prayers written by the Early Church. While the 1979 Book of Common Prayer contains a few modern novelties, such as Eucharistic Prayer

The Meaning and Symbols of Holy Eucharist

C, for the most part the prayers and liturgies are more ancient than even those in the 1662 Book of Common Prayer.

We will not here engage in the debate over different liturgies and prayer books. Eucharistic Prayer A from the 1979 Book of Common Prayer was chosen because it is familiar, and the most commonly used Eucharistic Prayer of the modern Anglican liturgies in the United States.

Throughout the rest of this study guide, the abbreviation "BCP" will be used to refer to the Book of Common Prayer, and usually referring to the 1979 Book of Common Prayer. Also, it should be noted that the term "catholic" means *universal*. It does not mean *Roman* Catholic, exclusively. Prior to 1054, the Catholic Church was united and included the Orthodox Church, the Roman Catholic Church, Celtic Catholics, and a number of other regional/ethnic catholic bodies that viewed themselves as part of the One Holy Catholic Church. When East and West fractured in 1054, the Roman Church assumed the place of ecclesiastical authority without the consultation or agreement of the other Catholic bodies. During the Reformation Movement and beyond, the Church of England strove to rediscover its ancient catholic origins, and to re-establish early christian practice, worship and beliefs. So, the use of the term "catholic" in this study guide intentionally refers to the Early Church.

The Meaning and Symbols of Holy Eucharist

The Real Presence

Consider therefore the Bread and the Wine not as bare elements, for they are, according to the Lord's declaration, the Body and Blood of Christ; for even though sense suggests this to thee, yet let faith establish thee. Judge not the matter from the taste, but from faith be fully assured without misgiving, that the Body and Blood of Christ have been vouchsafed to thee.

Saint Cyril of Jerusalem – *Catechetical Lectures*

Why is the Eucharist celebrated so often? The short answer is simply this: the Holy Eucharist is the center of our worship because Christ is the center of our worship.

We know that Jesus is present in many ways, places and times but those who view the Eucharist as a sacramental reality and not merely a symbol or memorial, find Jesus more profoundly real and present within the mystery of Holy Communion, than anywhere else. This is why the mystery of what happens during the prayers over the bread and wine has come to be called the Doctrine of the Real Presence. The fact that it is a mystery does not mean "that we can know nothing about [it]: it is only something that the mind cannot wholly know." [Frank Sheed, Theology and Sanity]

In other words, God has revealed this great mystery to us

The Meaning and Symbols of Holy Eucharist

in a tangible way (through scripture and through the creatures of bread and wine) so that we may be blessed by it, even though we do not completely understand it.

The 13th century theologian and teacher, Saint Thomas Aquinas went to great effort to define what was happening during the Eucharistic prayers, which he taught as the Doctrine of Transubstantiation. Though Saint Thomas has been often criticized as having defined the doctrine too narrowly, what he was expressing was his deep reverence and devotion for Christ's presence in the Eucharist. Saint Thomas would have been appalled at the idea that anyone should worship bread and wine. It was because he was convinced of Christ's genuine presence during the celebration of Holy Eucharist, that he was compelled to worship. In fact, after a celebration of the Holy Eucharist in December of 1273, Thomas was moved to say, "All I have written seems like straw compared to what I have seen and what has been revealed to me." After that experience, he ceased writing his masterwork, the Summa Theologica, and died a year later.

Personally, I think it unlikely that the doctrine of Transubstantiation overextends the doctrine of the Real Presence. More likely, it falls short of the real, unseen miracle. What I mean by this is that whatever reality St Thomas attempted to describe through his writings, that description cannot compare to the miracle that Christ actually presents at the Eucharist. I suggest this because it fits the nature and practices of Christ to be always more and love more and provide more of himself than we can completely grasp (compare Colossians 1:15-20).

The Meaning and Symbols of Holy Eucharist

Frankly, I yearn to see what it was that St Thomas saw during that December Mass in 1273. But I do not think that is possible for any of us, unless we are resolved to prayerfully devote ourselves to worship.

Recently, someone proposed the image of what an amazing experience it would be to suddenly see Jesus and to be able to touch him and worship him. My response (which I hope was not interpreted as flippant or arrogant) was that we do get to do that every time we come to the altar rail. What a shame if we do not recognize that. Consider the father's plea to Jesus, "I do believe; help me overcome my unbelief!" (Mark 9:24).

The liturgy, the architecture, the vestments and appointments are all designed to help us focus on Jesus' Real Presence. Recall how immediately following the great AMEN (BCP 363), which is the exulting assent of the Eucharistic Prayer, we pray the Lord's Prayer with the phrase, "give us this day our daily bread"! The Lord's Prayer is followed by the silent and dramatic Fraction (breaking of the priest host), recalling the disciples' experience with Jesus, when "the two told what had happened on the way, and how Jesus was recognized by them when he broke the bread" (Luke 24:35).

The silent pause after the Fraction invites us to take up our own prayer, "Lord be known to us in the breaking of the bread." The silence should fall heavy upon us as we realize that we are soon to hear the bittersweet proclamation, "Christ our Passover is Sacrificed for us" and the joyful invitation to come and receive our Lord, "The Gifts of God

The Meaning and Symbols of Holy Eucharist

for the People of God." Next, we encounter the greatest reality, this side of heaven.

Through Baptism we are immersed in Christ and clothed with Christ. Through the Holy Eucharist we consume Christ and are consumed by Christ, becoming Christ's Body to a broken and needy world.

Finally, a word about silence. After what we have just considered, how important is it to enjoy silence before you worship? I suggest to you that it is extremely important. We need to strive to find silence and prayer in anticipation of Holy Eucharist. I realize that our culture does not encourage this but all the more reason for us to invest in it. I invite you therefore, to prepare prayerfully on Saturday evening and to respect, participate and encourage prayerful silence as you enter the church. Because we are so happy to see one another (which is wonderful!), we often want to visit before the service. Instead, try to save that for afterwards or visit outside, so that you do not distract those who are in prayer for those brief fifteen minutes or so before the worship begins.

Further into this book, you will find some recommended guidelines and prayers to help you prepare for Holy Eucharist.

The Meaning and Symbols of Holy Eucharist

How to Receive Communion

On every Lord's Day—his special day—come together and break bread and give thanks, first confessing your sins so that your sacrifice may be pure. Anyone at variance with his neighbor must not join you, until they are reconciled, lest your sacrifice be defiled. For it was of this sacrifice that the Lord said, "Always and everywhere offer me a pure sacrifice; for I am a great King, says the Lord, and my name is marveled at by the nations."

The Teaching of the Twelve Apostles (The Didache)

The most important aspect of coming to Holy Communion is preparation. The Anglican Church does not require that a communicant make a private confession prior to coming to Communion. The popular instruction regarding making a private confession is: "All may. None must. Some should." Saint Paul directs the Christian "to examine himself before he eats of the bread and drinks the cup." This examination will likely reveal a need for repentance. Saturday might be a more useful day for preparation than those rushed minutes, (or seconds!) kneeling before the opening hymn. From this perspective, each Saturday becomes a weekly Lent, and each Sunday is a weekly Easter. (Similar preparation ought to be made anytime one comes to Holy Communion, as many churches offer daily Eucharists.)

Consider the Saturday collect from Morning Prayer:

The Meaning and Symbols of Holy Eucharist

Almighty God, who after the creation of the world rested from all your works and sanctified a day of rest for all your creatures: Grant that we, putting away all earthly anxieties, may be duly prepared for the service of your sanctuary, and that our rest here upon earth may be a preparation for the eternal rest promised to your people in heaven; through Jesus Christ our Lord. Amen. [BCP, 99]

One's preparation continues through a prayerful state of mind as one enters the church, noting the red doors that remind us of our entrance into the Church through the blood of Christ. Often, a font is in the Narthex, or near the interior doors of the church, where we can dip our fingers in holy water, making the sign of the cross on our foreheads to remind ourselves of the vows made at our baptisms.

Worshippers are urged to quietly find their seat so that they and others may enjoy the silence necessary for private prayers before the Liturgy begins. For those of you who are loquacious, please use the Narthex or Parish Hall for your conversations!

You will see throughout the Liturgy, that much of the Liturgy of the Word prepares us for receiving Holy Communion, especially the Collect for Purity, the Confession, and the Peace. The significance of these is described in the Instructed Eucharist, above.

After the the consecration of the bread and wine, the communicants are invited to the Altar rail (or station, if the communicants receive standing). Traditionally, the communicant comes to the Altar rail and kneels making the

The Meaning and Symbols of Holy Eucharist

sign of the cross. Congregations have different practices for the order in which they approach and fill the Altar rail. Observe those in front of you to discover the local practice, or wait for the usher to guide you. At the Altar rail, you may receive kneeling or standing. Those who have trouble or pain when kneeling should not kneel, and are encouraged to stand. Small children should stand up when being communicated. (This is very helpful to the clergy and ministers who have creaky backs!).

Only those who are baptized Christians may receive Holy Communion. Those who have not been baptized may come and cross their arms over their chests to indicate that they are not receiving Communion, but would like to receive a blessing.

Those who are receiving communion may receive in one kind: the Bread (the Host; the Body), or in two kinds: the Bread (the Body) and the Wine (the Blood). The Bread being the Body of Christ, (that is the Flesh) is understood to contain the Blood, and therefore is sufficient to receive alone without the Wine. This is why home communions and hospital communions often are only given in one kind – the Bread. Receiving in one kind may also be helpful for those who cannot tolerate alcohol. If you are gluten intolerant, let the priest know. Gluten-free wafers are available.

When receiving the Host (the Bread), lift up your hands with your right hand cupped in your left hand. Try to keep them level or the Host may slip out of your hand. If the Host falls onto the floor, leave it there. The priest will pick

The Meaning and Symbols of Holy Eucharist

it up and consume it and give you another Host. If for some reason the priest does not do this, then you must pick up the Host and reverently consume it. You may consume the Host immediately, or hold it in your hand to be dipped in the Wine by the Deacon (or Chalice Bearer). This latter method is called "intinction." After intinction, the Deacon will place the Host on your tongue. For intinction not to be awkward, you must hold your head straight, with your mouth wide open and your tongue stuck out as far as you are able, comfortably. I know that sounds strange, but it works. Otherwise, the deacon may accidentally touch your tongue with his fingers, or the Host may drop onto the floor. And the deacon definitely does not want to consume it after it falls out of your mouth, but will do it out of necessity. So please: head straight; mouth wide open; tongue straight out!

When receiving the Blood (the Wine), hold your hands up in the same manner: right hand over left. The deacon will present the Chalice to you, for you to guide. Place your hands under the base of the Chalice and guide it to your lips, releasing pressure when you are done. It is helpful for you to do this, because it is often difficult for the deacon to see whether or not you have received the Wine, (especially if women are wearing hats). The deacon will hold the Chalice in such a way that you may easily tilt it. You do not need to grip it or pull it. The Wine is to be sipped and not gulped.

If you are sick, please use intinction and do not drink from the Chalice. However, the church should be using a wine that has a stronger alcohol content than the typical table wine, (13%), such as cream sherry (18%). This is done to reduce the risk of communicating illness. This is also why the clergy SHOULD NOT add much water to the wine at the Altar.

Small children should also communicate in one kind, or by intinction. This begs the question of, "How old does someone have to be in order to receive Holy Communion?" I can't answer that for you here. You will need to ask your parish priest to explain the standard the he maintains. Traditionally, children are supposed to go through Confirmation and First Communion classes before they receive. Others, take the words of Jesus, "Allow the little children to come to me, do not hinder them" [Mark 10:14] as an invitation to even small children who are hungry for Jesus to receive communion, if they can do so respectfully.

It is traditional, but not necessary to make the sign of the cross after receiving each kind, and then to quietly exit the Altar rail. At a busy church where many people are being communicated it is easy to feel rushed. And, I fear the clergy are partly to blame for this as they are mindful of moving people along – especially if they have multiple services on Sunday. Even so, I urge you to take your time and to truly worship. This is the reason why you are worshipping in a Liturgical-Sacramental church – to be close to Jesus in a miraculous and mystical way – so take your time and linger there for a moment. It is after all His Table, not the priest's. Even if you are rushed, you will have time back at your pew to kneel and continue your devotions.

The Meaning and Symbols of Holy Eucharist

Ideally, our preparation for Holy Eucharist relates to our overall life or prayer, or a "rule of life" as some follow. For that reason, Anglicans are encouraged to pray the Daily Office, which includes Morning Prayer and Evening Prayer. Some also observe Noon Day prayers and Compline. Praying the Daily Offices can be a daunting process for those who are not familiar with it because there are so many rubrics and options. I have included guidelines as an aid to praying through Morning Prayer toward the end of this book.

CHAPTER FIVE

An Instructed Eucharist

Based on the American 1979 Book of Common Prayer

I have long been wishing, O true-born and dearly beloved children of the Church, to discourse to you concerning these spiritual and heavenly Mysteries; but since I well knew that seeing is far more persuasive than hearing, I waited for the present season; that finding you more open to the influence of my words from your present experience, I might lead you by the hand into the brighter and more fragrant meadow of the Paradise before us; especially as ye have been made fit to receive the more sacred Mysteries, after having been found worthy of divine and life-giving Baptism. Since therefore it remains to set before you a table of the more perfect instructions, let us now teach you these things exactly, that ye may know the effect wrought upon you on that evening of your baptism.

Saint Cyril of Jerusalem – *Catechetical Lectures*

The Meaning and Symbols of Holy Eucharist

This Instructed Eucharist is formatted presenting the text of the Book of Common Prayer first, followed by the commentary. Therefore the heading of the text is preceded by a capital letter, which corresponds to the commentary below it using the same capital letter. For example, "A. Rite" is descriptive of the heading of the Liturgy: "The Holy Eucharist: Rite Two". Below that heading is "A. Commentary" which provides the commentary for that segment of the Liturgy. Note: The text of the Book of Common Prayer is listed in serif, and the commentary in sanserif.

While this commentary corresponds specifically to the 1979 Book of Common Prayer used in much of the American Church, the elements are fairly universal, and it is hoped that it will be useful to those using other prayer books. Even though the order of the Liturgy and some of the headings have some minor differences between those of other Anglican prayer books, the reader will likely be able to recognize the corresponding section in his/her prayerbook. For example, prayer books used in the UK and other provinces, more commonly insert the General Confession at the beginning of the Liturgy rather than after the Prayers of the People, as found here. However, the commentary (P.) applies well in both cases.

The Meaning and Symbols of Holy Eucharist

A. Rite

The Holy Eucharist: Rite Two

A. Commentary: "Rite Two" refers to contemporary language. Rite One follows the same style of language used in earlier prayer books (thee, thou, thy), though not necessarily the same liturgical structure. For example, earlier prayer books begin with the corporate confession. Throughout the Rite, the reader will see brief instructions called *rubrics*. These rubrics were originally printed in red ink; now they are italicized.

B. Part One

The Word of God

B. Commentary: The Holy Eucharist is presented in two parts: the *Liturgy of the Word*, (The Word of God) and the *Liturgy of the Table* (The Holy Communion). This recognizes that Jesus is present in both Word and Sacrament.

C. Anthem

A hymn, psalm, or anthem may be sung

C. Commentary: "Anthem" is Anglican for "antiphon" and usually refers to scripture set to music. In some churches a verse of scripture is read and then a hymn is sung.

D. Salutation

The Celebrant   Blessed be God: Father, Son, and Holy Spirit.

People And blessed be his kingdom, now and forever. Amen.

D. Commentary: This is a Trinitarian acclamation. The Catholic proclamation of the doctrine of the Holy Trinity is evident throughout the Liturgy. Options are also given for Easter and Lenten salutations.

E. The Collect for Purity
The Celebrant may say

Almighty God, to you all hearts are open, all desires known, and from you no secrets are hid: Cleanse the thoughts of our hearts by the inspiration of your Holy Spirit, that we may perfectly love you, and worthily magnify your holy Name; through Christ our Lord. Amen.

E. Commentary: We petition God to prepare us and purify us so that we may enter into His Holy Presence with clean hearts. A penitential order is available as an optional introduction, which includes the corporate confession. The Penitential Order is most appropriate for Lent. [BCP 351] For the meaning of "collect", see "G", below.

The Meaning and Symbols of Holy Eucharist

F. Gloria
When appointed, the following hymn or some other song of praise is sung or said, all standing

Glory to God in the highest,
and peace to his people on earth.
Lord God, heavenly King,
almighty God and Father,
we worship you, we give you thanks,
we praise you for your glory.
Lord Jesus Christ, only Son of the Father,
Lord God, Lamb of God,
you take away the sin of the world:
have mercy on us;
you are seated at the right hand of the Father:
receive our prayer.
For you alone are the Holy One,
you alone are the Lord,
you alone are the Most High,
Jesus Christ,
with the Holy Spirit,
in the glory of God the Father. Amen.

F. Commentary: The Gloria. The purpose of all worship is to glorify God. The Gloria placed at the beginning of the Liturgy helps to emphasize the central purpose of worship as bringing glory to God our first priority.

G. The Collect of the Day

Celebrant   The Lord be with you.
People   And also with you.
Celebrant   Let us pray.

O God, you have taught us to keep all your commandments by loving you and our neighbor: Grant us the grace of your Holy Spirit, that we may be devoted to you with our whole heart, and united to one another with pure affection; through Jesus Christ our Lord, who lives and reigns with you and the Holy Spirit, one God, for ever and ever. Amen.

G. Commentary: The Collect of the Day. There is a different opening collect for each Sunday and Feast Day. This collect comes from Proper 9. In Anglicanism the word "Collect" is pronounced with a short "o" and the emphasis is on the first syllable. But the meaning is as it appears. It simply means that it is a prayer to gather or collect the prayers of the people under one unified theme. Ideally, it reflects the theme of the lessons, season, or feast day. The contemporary collects begin on page 211 of BCP. [See also Structure of Collects, below.]

H. The Lessons

The people sit.

The Meaning and Symbols of Holy Eucharist

After each Reading, the Lector may say,
The Word of the Lord.

People may respond, Thanks be to God.

H. Commentary: The focal point of the Liturgy of the Word is the Lessons, the heart of which is the Gospel. It is important to note that it is the reading of God's word and especially the words of Christ that receive the most honor NOT the preacher and the sermon. This is why the Gospel is processed into the congregation held high by the deacon. Elevating and reading the Gospel during the Liturgy of the Word is equivalent to the elevation and blessing of the bread and wine during the Liturgy of the Table, which, by the way, is made present by the words of Christ and the invoking of the Holy Spirit. Similarly, the Celebrant (priest or bishop) prays over the head of the deacon invoking the Holy Spirit to empower the reading of the Gospel before the deacon carries the Gospel into the congregation.

The Lectionary is divided into three years. The first year (A) leads with the Gospel of Matthew, the second year (B) with Mark, and the third year (C) with Luke. John's Gospel takes center stage during Lent and Easter in all three years. The Gospel accords with the theme of the day, season or feast day. Sometimes the

The Meaning and Symbols of Holy Eucharist

Old Testament lesson or New Testament lesson correspond to the gospel, but not always. On certain major feast days, the lessons all correspond. See August 6th and the Feast of the Transfiguration, for an example [BCP 924].

I. Psalm

I. Commentary: In keeping with the Benedictine structure used in the Daily Offices, the reading of Scripture is followed by a canticle, Psalm or hymn. While not always the case, traditionally, we kneel to pray, sit to listen and stand to praise.

J. Gradual Hymn

J. Commentary: In the case of the "gradual hymn" offered before the Gospel, we are not so much standing to sing, as we are standing to honor Christ in the proclamation of the Gospel, which the Gospel Book represents. So, when we stand for the Gospel and bow as the cross passes by we are honoring the One whom they represent.

K. The Gospel

Deacon The Holy Gospel of our Lord Jesus Christ according to . . .

K. Commentary: Jesus is present in Word and Sacrament. The deacon declaring the Gospel is the climax of the Liturgy of the Word. The elevation of the Gospel during the Liturgy of the Word equates to the elevation of the Sacrament during the Liturgy of the Table. Both the deacon and the celebrant represent Jesus to the gathered community during these two pinnacles.

The practice of crossing one's forehead, lips and heart at the announcement of the Gospel may have a number of traditional meanings, but the following seems most appropriate: It is a silent prayer asking the Lord to instruct our mind, embolden our speech, and transform our hearts, as we hear the words of Jesus.

L. The Sermon

L. Commentary: As noted previously, reading the Gospel is the focal point of the Liturgy of the Word. The preacher's responsibility is to submit to the Word just read, and to preach and teach as one in submission to the Word of God. Therefore, the preacher may only preach on the lessons. Occasionally the preacher may preach on the collect, or season of the day, in so far as they correspond to the theme of the lessons. As much as we like novelty, the preacher is required to teach only those things which accord with Scripture, and received Apostolic Tradition.

M. The Nicene Creed

We believe in one God, the Father, the Almighty, maker of heaven and earth, of all that is, seen and unseen.

We believe in one Lord, Jesus Christ, the only Son of God, eternally begotten of the Father, God from God, Light from Light, true God from true God, begotten, not made, of one Being with the Father. Through him all things were made. For us and for our salvation he came down from heaven: by the power of the Holy Spirit he became incarnate from the Virgin Mary, and was made man. For our sake he was crucified under Pontius Pilate; he suffered death and was buried. On the third day he rose again in accordance with the Scriptures; he ascended into heaven and is seated at the right hand of the Father. He will come again in glory to judge the living and the dead, and his kingdom will have no end.

We believe in the Holy Spirit, the Lord, the giver of life, who proceeds from the Father and the Son. With the Father and the Son he is worshiped and glorified. He has spoken through the Prophets. We believe in one holy catholic and apostolic Church. We acknowledge one baptism for the forgiveness of sins. We look for the resurrection of the dead, and the life of the world to come. Amen.

M. Commentary: There are three creeds: the Apostles Creed which is used in the Daily Offices, the Nicene Creed which is used during Holy Eucharist, and the Creed of Athanasius, which is no longer used in the 1979 BCP liturgies, but may be found in the Historical Documents on p. 864. All of these creeds proclaim the work of the Trinity and especially to make clear the incarnation of the Son of God. See also the Definition of Chalcedon [BCP 864]. The Creeds placement after the sermon serves as a corrective to any poor teaching given by the preacher.

The Creed is said standing, as we the Church publicly proclaim our belief in the Triune God. Other prayer books present the Creed in first person singular: "I believe" to emphasize the personal responsibility of every Christian to proclaim his/her Faith.

The Nicene Creed in the 1979 BCP includes the Filioque Statement, which is the phrase "and the Son" in the third segment of the Creed describing the Holy Spirit proceeding from the Father. The Filioque Statement was added in the sixth century but not authorized by the Pope until eleventh century. The Filioque was not present in the original Nicene Creed.

The Meaning and Symbols of Holy Eucharist

The insertion of that phrase by the Western Church is one of the issues that led to the Great Schism between the Western Church and the Eastern Church in 1054. The controversy surrounds the value placed on the full equality of each member of the Trinity. While the Lambeth Counsel and Conventions of the Episcopal Church have declared that the Filioque Statement be removed from the Nicene Creed, it has yet to be taken out of the prayer books. The inclusion of the Filioque Statement continues to be an obstacle to ecumenical relations with the Orthodox Church.

It is customary to bow at the mention of the Incarnation, recognizing the unfathomable humility of Christ as Saint Paul described in Philippians chapter 2. It is also traditional to cross one's self at the mention of the "resurrection of the dead".

O. The Prayers of the People

Prayer is offered with intercession for

The Universal Church, its members, and its mission
The Nation and all in authority
The welfare of the world
The concerns of the local community
Those who suffer and those in any trouble
The departed (with commemoration of a saint when appropriate)

See the forms beginning on page 383.

The Meaning and Symbols of Holy Eucharist

If there is no celebration of the Communion, or if a priest is not available, the service is concluded as directed on page 406.

O. Commentary: Ideally, the Prayers of the People are offered by a deacon as the one who best personifies the Church to being in the World but not of the World. The prayers begin with the Universal Church and the world and conclude with those known to us personally. Several forms for prayers are given (but not required) beginning on page 383 of BCP.

P. Confession of Sin

The Deacon says,
Let us confess our sins against God and our neighbor.

Silence may be kept.

Minister and People
Most merciful God, we confess that we have sinned against you in thought, word, and deed, by what we have done, and by what we have left undone. We have not loved you with our whole heart; we have not loved our neighbors as ourselves. We are truly sorry and we humbly repent. For the sake of your Son Jesus Christ, have mercy on us and forgive us; that we may delight in your will, and walk in your ways, to the glory of your Name. Amen.

The Priest, stands and says,

Almighty God have mercy on you, forgive you all your sins through our Lord Jesus Christ, strengthen you in all goodness, and by the power of the Holy Spirit keep you in eternal life. *Amen.*

P. Commentary: This is a corporate confession. Corresponding to the deacon leading the assembly in corporate prayer, next the deacon leads the Body in corporate confession. The people as a whole are confessing that they have failed to represent Christ to the World as we ought. The Church is responsible for living out the Great Commandment and fulfilling the Great Commission, but we recognize that we have fallen short of this. The confession for individual sin may be offered privately using the form on page 447. Personal sins against one's neighbor may also be reconciled during the Peace. [See Q. below]

Q. The Peace

Q. Commentary: In the Early Church the "Kiss of Peace" (a holy kiss), was a common form of greeting found in the New Testament [Romans 16.16; 2 Corinthians 13.12; 1 Peter 5.14] The purpose for offering the peace might well be understood by the (offertory) scripture from Matthew 5.23, 24 "If you are offering your gift at the altar, and there remember that your brother has something against you, leave your gift there before the altar and go; first be reconciled to your brother, and then come and offer your gift." (See also Matthew 18.15-19). The peace should not be used as an intermission or brief fellowship event. The Peace is placed here in the Liturgy between the Confession and the Offertory as a means for the gathered Christians to ensure that there are no causes for division between them, before coming to Communion. In other words, the person most deserving of your peace, would be the one with whom you have had a disagreement. The Peace provides the opportunity for us to evaluate the health of our relationships with one another [1 Corinthians 11.17-34].

Then the Deacon cries aloud, "Receive ye one another; and let us kiss one another." Think not that this kiss is of the same character with those given in public by common friends. It is not such: but this kiss blends souls one with another, and courts entire forgiveness for them. The kiss therefore is the sign that our souls are mingled together, and banish all remembrance of wrongs. For this cause Christ said, If thou art offering thy gift at the altar, and there rememberest that thy brother hath aught against time, leave there thy gift upon the altar, and go thy way; first be reconciled to thy brother, and then come and offer thy gift.

The Meaning and Symbols of Holy Eucharist

The kiss therefore is reconciliation, and for this reason holy: as the blessed Paul somewhere cried, saying, Greet ye one another with a holy kiss; and Peter, with a kiss of charity.
                    Saint Cyril of Jerusalem – *Catechetical Lectures*

The Holy Communion

R. The Offertory

R. Commentary: The Offertory marks the transition from the Liturgy of the Word and the Liturgy of the Table. The activity and focus of worship moves from the Nave to the Sanctuary. A Song of Ascents might come to mind at this moment. [Psalms 120 - 134]

The altar is on a raised platform. Not so that it can be seen more easily but to help us enter into heavenly worship with angels and archangels. Christ is high and lifted up. (See Isaiah 52.13, and John 12.32, below) Worship in Scripture is associated with the high places, which is emblematic of the heavenly throne room. (See Hebrews 8.5, below) The celebrant puts on a chasuble as a symbol of the glory cloud descending on the tabernacle and filling it with God's glory. The vestments, vessels, and stained glass windows are beautiful as an aid to think, pray and worship in terms of heavenly glory. The idea that these emblems are idolatrous is a misunderstanding of their symbolic function. The celebrant (priest) does not wear vestments to bring attention to himself but to obliterate his individuality and to point to the glory of God.

Isaiah 52:13
Behold, my servant shall act wisely; he shall be high and lifted up, and shall be exalted.

John 12:32
And I, when I am lifted up from the earth, will draw all people to myself."

Hebrews 8:5
They serve a copy and shadow of the heavenly things. For when Moses was about to erect the tent, he was instructed by God, saying, "See that you make everything according to the pattern that was shown you on the mountain."

The Offertory Sentences are found on pages 376, 377 of the BCP.

Preparing the Table: During the offertory, the deacon prepares the Table and the Celebrant prepares himself through ablutions, praying Psalm 26:6-8. The deacon pours in a small amount of blessed water into the wine, which reminds us of the water and the blood that flowed from Jesus' pierced side. This is emblematic of our baptism in Jesus' blood for the forgiveness of our sins, and our baptism by the Holy Spirit for our Sanctification and gifting for ministry. (See John 19.34, below). This practice began in the early Church as simply a practical method of diluting concentrated wine. In this we see how the Church over time attributed a theological significance to something that was merely pragmatic.

John 19:34
But one of the soldiers pierced his side with a spear, and at once there came out blood and water.

The Great Thanksgiving

Eucharistic Prayer A

1. The Celebrant

The people remain standing. The Celebrant, whether bishop or priest, faces them and sings or says

1. Commentary: In Morning Prayer the title of the one who leads the prayers is "officiant". The term "celebrant" indicates the fact that the Eucharist is a celebration. It is a memorial of Christ's death, resurrection and ascension. And it is a thanksgiving to be celebrated because of Christ's victory over death and the life that he offers to us through his flesh and blood. The Church of England's alternative liturgies found in the A.D. 2000 book of Common Worship employs the term "president" rather than "celebrant" as the one who presides at the Holy Table. In the United States, the term "celebrant" is to be preferred, as the term "president" is overly encumbered by both political and secular associations.

2. The Sursum Corda

Celebrant　The Lord be with you.
People　　And also with you.
Celebrant　Lift up your hearts.
People　　We lift them to the Lord.
Celebrant　Let us give thanks to the Lord our God.
People　　It is right to give him thanks and praise.

2. Commentary: The exchange above between the celebrant and the people is known as the "sursum corda" which is Latin for "lift up your hearts." The Sursum Corda proclaims that we are not only offering the gifts that God has given us back to Him (as evidenced by bread and wine), but that we are offering what is most precious – our hearts to Him.

After this the Priest cries aloud, "Lift up your hearts." For truly ought we in that most awful hour to have our heart on high with God, and not below, thinking of earth and earthly things. In effect therefore the Priest bids all in that hour to dismiss all cares of this life, or household anxieties, and to have their heart in heaven with the merciful God. Then ye answer, "We lift them up unto the Lord:" assenting to it, by your avowal. But let no one come here, who could say with his mouth, "We lift up our hearts unto the Lord," but in his thoughts have his mind concerned with the cares of this life. At all times, rather, God should be in our memory but if this is impossible by reason of human infirmity, in that hour above all this should be our earnest endeavour.

Saint Cyril of Jerusalem – *Catechetical Lectures*

3. Facing East

Then, facing the Holy Table, the Celebrant proceeds

3. Commentary: Traditionally the celebrant stands at the Holy Table facing *east* while praying to God and facing *west* while addressing God's people. This rubric assumes that the celebrant is standing between the people and the Altar, where the Altar is against the east wall of the church. Praying "eastward" demonstrates our expectation for the promised return of Christ. Prayer and worship is directed toward God (liturgically eastward) and de-emphasizes any resemblance to a performance on a stage directed toward the people as entertainment. However, the priest who celebrates at the altar facing the people, is seen as an example of Jesus presiding at the Last Supper facing his disciples. This practice embraces the idea of intimate table fellowship, and reminds us of Jesus referring to his disciples as "friends" [John 15.15]. Don't you face your friends at a meal? Whichever practice you cling to, remember that the goal is to honor Christ. Such preferences must never be used to divide or polarize members of Christ's Church.

After the celebrant has put on the chasuble and taken his place at the altar, he is no longer to be thought of or noticed as our familiar friend and pastor. With fear and trepidation he assumes the visible role *in persona Christi* who stands as an emblem of Christ during the Last Supper, as he speaks the words of Christ during the prayer of consecration. Any notion on the part of the celebrant, or others around him, that he personally is somehow Christ enfleshed is a grave and idolatrous mistake. The celebrant merely and humbly offers the words of Christ in recognizable form, petitioning the Spirit to do as Christ wills.

4. Thanksgiving

It is right, and a good and joyful thing, always and everywhere to give thanks to you, Father Almighty, Creator of heaven and earth.

The Meaning and Symbols of Holy Eucharist

4. Commentary: The preface opens with a proclamation of thanksgiving. "Eucharist" means "thanksgiving".

5. Proper Preface
Here a Proper Preface is sung or said on all Sundays, and on other occasions as appointed.

5. Commentary: The Proper Preface may be found in BCP pages 377-382 and changes according to the season or day.

6. With Angels and Archangels
Therefore we praise you, joining our voices with Angels and Archangels and with all the company of heaven, who for ever sing this hymn to proclaim the glory of your Name:

6. Commentary: The preface closes with the recognition that worship on earth is a reflection of the worship in heaven. Scriptural precedence for "Joining our voices with Angels and Archangels" can be found in Psalm 148:1-2 and Revelation 5:11-12.

7. Sanctus
Holy, holy, holy Lord, God of power and might, heaven and earth are full of your glory. Hosanna in the highest. Blessed is he who comes in the name of the Lord. Hosanna in the highest.

The Meaning and Symbols of Holy Eucharist

7. Commentary: The Latin for "Holy" is Sanctus. [Revelation 4:7] It is traditional to cross one's self at the phrase "Blessed is he who comes . . ." See Psalm 118:26 and Matthew 21:9

8. Prayer Posture
The people stand or kneel.

8. Commentary: The tradition of standing during the Eucharistic Prayer originates with the Orthodox Church and kneeling with the Roman Church. Anglicanism draws from both traditions and either posture is appropriate.

9. Institution Narrative Preface
Holy and gracious Father: In your infinite love you made us for yourself; and, when we had fallen into sin and become subject to evil and death, you, in your mercy, sent Jesus Christ, your only and eternal Son, to share our human nature, to live and die as one of us, to reconcile us to you, the God and Father of all.

He stretched out his arms upon the cross, and offered himself in obedience to your will, a perfect sacrifice for the whole world.

9. Commentary: Before the words of the Last Supper are uttered, we are reminded of why Jesus' sacrifice was necessary. God's holy nature, humanity's fallen nature and God's plan of salvation are recalled in a beautifully concise summary.

10. Manual Acts

At the following words concerning the bread, the Celebrant is to hold it or lay a hand upon it; and at the words concerning the cup, to hold or place a hand upon the cup and any other vessel containing wine to be consecrated.

10. Commentary: The celebrant employs "manual acts" that function practically to place the bread, wine and vessels in their proper places but also as a way to gesture through the prayer in a way that reflects what is being prayed, while not being novel or distracting. The celebrant's vestments and gestures must draw the worshipers hearts and minds toward Christ and not the priest. The priest's identity should be obscured by the image of Christ. Likewise, when Christians cross themselves or genuflect, they are proclaiming and teaching what they believe about the reality and sovereignty of Christ and their adoration for him as their Lord. We proclaim our faith by both word and deed. 1 Cor. 11:26, "For as often as you eat this bread and drink the cup, you proclaim the Lord's death until he comes." The celebrant may also incorporate "secret" prayers during the manual acts, examples of which are found in chapter six.

11. Institution Narrative – Last Supper Remembered

On the night he was handed over to suffering and death, our Lord Jesus Christ took bread; and when he had given thanks to you, he broke it, and gave it to his disciples, and said, "Take, eat: This is my Body, which is given for you. Do this for the remembrance of me."

After supper he took the cup of wine; and when he had given thanks, he gave it to them, and said, "Drink this, all of you: This is my Blood of the new Covenant, which is shed for you and for many for the forgiveness of sins. Whenever you drink it, do this for the remembrance of me."

11. Commentary: Ironically, "the Last Supper" is the first of countless Suppers where Christ is remembered, honored and received with renewing life each time He is celebrated.

Christ *took* bread. Gave *thanks*. *Broke* the bread and *gave* it to the disciples. This four-fold action is recalled in the words and ceremony of the Eucharist. The words beginning with "On the night . . ." and "After supper . . ." are the Prayers of Consecration, being the words of Christ directly quoted from the Gospels and 1 Corinthians 11:23-26. The doctrine of

The Meaning and Symbols of Holy Eucharist

the Real Presence of Christ in the Eucharist is not realized because of magical powers by the priest but is realized through the words of Christ spoken in remembrance of Him. [Note John 1:1-18 & Genesis 1.] God's creative power is through the Word. "Remembrance" (Greek = *anamnesis*) in the ancient world was not simply a mental reflection but was the actual re-membering of a person into one's presence. [Note John 6:53-55] So Jesus said to them, "Truly, truly, I say to you, unless you eat the flesh of the Son of Man and drink his blood, you have no life in you. Whoever feeds on my flesh and drinks my blood has eternal life, and I will raise him up on the last day. For my flesh is true food, and my blood is true drink."

The elevation of the blessed bread and wine at the conclusion of Christ's words of blessing are not only for the sake of honoring Christ, but also to remind us that through our baptism into Christ, God now views us through the body and blood of Jesus - as redeemed by Him.

We thank thee, our Father, for the holy vine of David Thy servant, which Thou madest known to us through Jesus Thy Servant; to Thee be the glory for ever. And concerning the broken bread: We thank Thee, our Father, for the life and knowledge which Thou madest known to us through Jesus Thy Servant; to Thee be the glory for ever. Even as this broken bread was scattered over the hills, and was gathered together and became one, so let Thy Church be gathered together from the ends of the earth into Thy kingdom; for Thine is the glory and the power through Jesus Christ for ever.

The Teaching of the Twelve Apostles

12. Memorial Acclamation

Therefore we proclaim the mystery of faith:

Celebrant and People

Christ has died.
Christ is risen.
Christ will come again.

We celebrate the memorial of our redemption, O Father, in this sacrifice of praise and thanksgiving. Recalling his death, resurrection, and ascension, we offer you these gifts.

12. Commentary: In case there was any doubt about what was proclaimed earlier in the Creed, the worshipers boldly claim that Christ has conquered death and will return to bring about his complete victory. The fact of which, is something to be remembered and celebrated.

13. Epiclesis

Sanctify them by your Holy Spirit to be for your people the Body and Blood of your Son, the holy food and drink of new and unending life in him. Sanctify us also that we may faithfully receive this holy Sacrament, and serve you in unity, constancy, and peace; and at the last day bring us with all your saints into the joy of your eternal kingdom.

13. Commentary: *Epiclesis* refers to petitioning the Holy Spirit to descend upon the creatures of bread and wine to set them apart as the Holy Body and Blood of Christ [Cp. Genesis 1:2 and Luke 1:35]. "Sanctify" means to "set apart" from common use, for God's use.

The celebrant may indicate the epiclesis by the sign of the cross and hands descending and covering the consecrated bread and wine. Anglican sacramental theology holds the consecration of the elements to be a Holy Mystery made present through the words of Christ and the work of the Holy Spirit. Where the epiclesis follows the Institution Narrative (words of Christ), the act of consecration is seen as a two-fold blessing occurring from the words of Christ (11) and through the epiclesis (13) and affirmed by the worshipers at the Great Amen.

Here, the epiclesis is immediately followed by the benediction: "Sanctify us . . ." as a corresponding oblation (offering) of the worshippers' selves (Cp. Offertory) to be made ready to receive the Sanctifed Gifts that the people presented at the Offertory. In like manner to the Celebrant making the sign of the Cross over the Gifts, it is traditional to cross one's self at this benediction.

In Liturgies where the epiclesis comes before the Institution Narrative (the words of Christ), as in the 1549 BCP and Common Worship (2000, UK), the epiclesis functions as a sanctifying invocation to make the bread and wine ready for the consecrating words of Christ. Correspondingly, the Institution Narrative is then followed by an invocation (benediction) for the people of God to be made ready to receive the Holy Food. Note how the epiclesis and the benediction frame (see bracketed notes) the Narrative in this excerpt from the 1549 Book of Common Prayer (Archbishop Thomas Cranmer),

> *O God heavenly father, which of thy tender mercie diddest geve thine only sonne Jesu Christ to suffre death upon the crosse for our redempcion, who made there (by his one oblacion once offered) a full, perfect, and sufficient sacrifyce, oblacion, and satysfaccyon, for the sinnes of the whole worlde, and did institute, and in his holy Gospell commaund us, to celebrate a perpetuall memory of that his*

precious death, untyll his comming again:

[Epiclesis] *Heare us (O merciful father) we besech thee; and with thy holy spirite and worde, vouchsafe to blesse and sanctifie these thy gyftes, and creatures of bread and wyne, that they maie be unto us the bodye and bloude of thy moste derely beloved sonne Jesus Christe.*

[Narrative] *Who in the same nyght that he was betrayed: tooke breade, and when he had blessed, and geven thankes: he brake it, and gave it to his disciples, saiyng: Take, eate, this is my bodye which is geven for you, do this in remembraunce of me.*

Likewyse after supper he toke the cuppe, and when he had geven thankes, he gave it to them, saiyng: drynk ye all of this, for this is my bloude of the newe Testament, whyche is shed for you and for many, for remission of synnes: do this as oft as you shall drinke it, in remembraunce of me.

[Rubrics for manual acts] *Here the priest must take the bread into his handes. Here the priest shall take the Cuppe into his handes.*

These wordes before rehersed are to be saied, turning still to the Altar, without any elevacion, or shewing the Sacrament to the people.

WHERFORE, O Lorde and heavenly father,

The Meaning and Symbols of Holy Eucharist

accordyng to the Instytucyon of thy derely beloved sonne, our saviour Jesu Christ, we thy humble servauntes do celebrate, and make here before thy divine Majestie, with these thy holy giftes, the memoryall whyche thy sonne hath wylled us to make, havyng in remembraunce his blessed passion, mightie resurreccyon, and gloryous ascencion, renderyng unto thee most hartie thankes, for the innumerable benefites procured unto us by the same, entierely desiryng thy fatherly goodnes, mercifully to accepte this our Sacrifice of praise and thankesgeving: most humbly beseching thee to graunt, that by the merites and death of thy sonne Jesus Christ, and through faith in his bloud, we and al thy whole church, may obteigne remission of our sinnes, and all other benefites of hys passyon.

[Benediction] *And here wee offre and present unto thee (O Lorde) oure selfe, oure soules, and bodies, to be a reasonable, holy, and lively sacrifice unto thee: humbly besechyng thee, that whosoever shalbee partakers of thys holy Communion, maye worthely receive the most precious body and bloude of thy sonne Jesus Christe: and bee fulfilled with thy grace and heavenly benediccion, and made one bodye with thy sonne Jesu Christe, that he maye dwell in them, and they in hym. And although we be unworthy (through our manyfolde synnes) to offre unto thee any Sacryfice: Yet we beseche thee to accepte thys our bounden duetie and service, and commaunde these our prayers and* *supplicacions, by the Ministery of thy holy Angels, to be brought up into thy holy Tabernacle before the syght of thy dyvine majestie; not waiyng our merites, but pardonyng our offences, through Christe our Lorde, by whome, and with whome, in the unitie of the holy Ghost: all honour and glory, be unto thee, O father almightie, world without ende. Amen.*

14. The Great Amen

All this we ask through your Son Jesus Christ. By him, and with him, and in him, in the unity of the Holy Spirit all honor and glory is yours, Almighty Father, now and for ever. AMEN.

14. Commentary: "All this we ask . . ." Again, the miracle of the Eucharist is recognized as the work of Christ in concert with the Holy Trinity; it is *not* by the work or words of the priest.

The Great Amen is the only amen in all capital letters. Why? "Amen" is a statement of agreement. The capital letters are to remind us of the great gift presented to us through Christ's redeeming presence. So, we agree boldly with voiced recognition of that Gift - AMEN!

15. The Lord's Prayer

And now, as our Savior Christ has taught us, we are bold to say,

Our Father, who art in heaven,
hallowed be thy Name,
thy kingdom come,
thy will be done,
on earth as it is in heaven.
Give us this day our daily bread.
And forgive us our trespasses,
as we forgive those
who trespass against us.
And lead us not into temptation,
but deliver us from evil.
For thine is the kingdom,
and the power, and the glory,
for ever and ever. Amen.

15. Commentary: Matthew 6:9-13. "Give us this day our daily bread" is a prayer for our daily needs but it is also a prayer for the continual presence of Christ in our lives. Literally, the phrase could be translated "give us this day the bread that comes upon us" echoing Jesus' proclamation in John 6:51, "I am the living bread that came down from heaven"

Prayer of Humble Access. In Rite One of the 1979 BCP, (as well as 1549, 1928 BCPs and 2000 Common Worship), the prayer called the "Prayer of Humble Access" follows the Lord's Prayer:

> *WE do not presume to come to this thy Table, O merciful Lord, trusting in our own righteousness, but in thy manifold and great mercies. We are not worthy so much as to gather up the crumbs under thy Table. But thou art the same Lord, whose property is always to have mercy: Grant us therefore, gracious Lord, so to eat the flesh of thy dear Son Jesus Christ, and to drink his blood, that our sinful bodies may be made clean by his body, and our souls washed through his most precious blood, and that we may evermore dwell in him, and he in us. Amen.* [1928 BCP]

In the 1662 BCP, the Prayer of Humble Access precedes the Prayer of Consecration (Institution Narrative).

16. The Fraction

The Celebrant breaks the consecrated Bread.

A period of silence is kept.

16. Commentary: "Not one of his bones will be broken." [Jn 19:36, Ex 12:46 & Ps 34:20.] Jesus as the Passover Lamb was prophesied to not have any bones broken. He was scourged and pierced but his bones were never broken. He remained the faultless paschal lamb to the very end. The breaking of the bread (or Fraction) recalls for us the fact that Jesus was the host at the Last Supper who broke the bread and gave it to his disciples. Also, the Eucharist on the way to Emmaus [Luke 24:13-35], "the two told what happened on the way, and how Jesus was recognized by them when he broke the bread."

After the fraction, you may see the curious action of the priest breaking off a piece of the Blessed Bread and drop it into the Chalice. This reminds the priest that he is serving under the bishop's authority. It is believed that in the early Church the bishop would drop a piece of consecrated bread into the consecrated wine that the deacon would be taking out to commune others who were not at the bishop's celebration. This was a sign to them that the Communion came from the bishop and it was a sign of unity. On Maundy Thursday, the celebrant places a fragment (Fermentum) from the Host consecrated by the Bishop during the Mass of Chrism.

"Silence is kept."
The breaking of the bread also reminds us of the tearing in two of the Temple curtain when Jesus gave up his spirit on the cross and opened access to the Holy Place (Matthew 27:50-54, Hebrews 10:19-22).

Therefore, we observe awe-filled silence along with the centurion who proclaimed, "Surely he was the Son of God!"

17. Fraction Anthem

[Alleluia.] Christ our Passover is sacrificed for us; Therefore let us keep the feast. [Alleluia.]

In Lent, Alleluia is omitted, and may be omitted at other times except during Easter Season.

In place of, or in addition to, the preceding, some other suitable anthem may be used.

17. Commentary: The silence is broken by the call to celebrate the heavenly feast. [Revelation 5:5-14; 19:6-9.]

18. The Celebrant Returns to Earth

Facing the people, the Celebrant says the following Invitation

The Gifts of God for the People of God.

and may add

Take them in remembrance that Christ died for you, and feed on him in your hearts by faith, with thanksgiving.

The Meaning and Symbols of Holy Eucharist

18. Commentary: The consecration of the people and the bread and wine is completed. The celebrant turns away from Liturgical East with his attention focused in prayer to the Father, and now addresses the community, announcing that the Heavenly Banquet is prepared and the feasting is about to begin.

19. Communion
The ministers receive the Sacrament in both kinds, and then immediately deliver it to the people.

The Bread and the Cup are given to the communicants with these words

The Body (Blood) of our Lord Jesus Christ keep you in everlasting life. [Amen.]

or with these words
The Body of Christ, the bread of heaven. [Amen.]
The Blood of Christ, the cup of salvation. [Amen.]

During the ministration of Communion, hymns, psalms, or anthems may be sung.

The Meaning and Symbols of Holy Eucharist

19. Commentary: In the Anglican Communion the Communion Table is open to all people who have been baptized in the name of the Father and the Son and the Holy Spirit. This form of administration emphasizes the Mystery of the Real Presence [See John 6:33-58]. The couplets "The Body of Christ, the bread of heaven" and "The Blood of Christ, the cup of salvation" allow some latitude for both a Catholic and Reformed theology: the "Body" and "Blood" for the Real Presence; the "bread" and "cup" for signification. These versicles are fine examples of the Elizabethan Settlement, which provided language that was intended to be acceptable to those in her realm who wanted Catholicism restored, and to those who wanted catholic practices and doctrine removed. However, we would do well to turn our attention away from debates over the "correct" descriptions of what happens at the altar and focus on the transformational reality of receiving Christ physically and spiritually. Receiving Christ at the Eucharist is not only worship, but it is a means for his Body and Blood to enrich our well-being in his family. This is a new eternal family status – new blood – which began at our baptism/conversion when we were regenerated and became a new creation [Mark 3:33-35; Romans 6:3-11; 2 Cor. 5:17; Eph. 4:24; Phil. 3:20-21; Col. 3:9-11]. The implication being that our feeding on him is so much more than just a symbolic memorial but a full participation in who Jesus is and who He is causing us to be: God's children, and children who are maturing.

John Donne (or Queen Elizabeth I) is credited with this simple but profound poem, which helps to express the Anglican understanding of The Real Presence:
God the Word, He spake it. Christ the Bread, He break it. What the Word doth make it. That I receive and take it.

20. Post-Communion Prayer

After Communion, the Celebrant says

Let us pray.

Celebrant and People

Eternal God, heavenly Father, you have graciously accepted us as living members of your Son our Savior Jesus Christ, and you have fed us with spiritual food in the Sacrament of his Body and Blood. Send us now into the world in peace, and grant us strength and courage to love and serve you with gladness and singleness of heart; through Christ our Lord. Amen.

20. Commentary: A Post-communion Prayer appears to be present in the Liturgy by the early second century, or at least by the early third century. The current post-communion prayer serves to remind us of the connection between the Dominical Sacraments:

The Meaning and Symbols of Holy Eucharist

Baptism and Holy Communion, and our responsibility to fulfill the Great Commandment and Great Commission.

But after ye are filled, thus give thanks: We thank Thee, holy Father, for Thy holy name which Thou didst cause to tabernacle in our hearts, and for the knowledge and faith and immortality, which Thou madest known to us through Jesus Thy Servant; to Thee be the glory for ever. Thou, Master almighty, didst create all things for Thy name's sake; Thou gavest food and drink to men for enjoyment, that they might give thanks to Thee; but to us Thou didst freely give spiritual food and drink and life eternal through Thy Servant. Before all things we thank Thee that Thou art mighty; to Thee be the glory for ever. Remember, Lord, Thy Church, to deliver it from all evil and to make it perfect in Thy love, and gather it from the four winds, sanctified for Thy kingdom which Thou hast prepared for it; for Thine is the power and the glory for ever. Let grace come, and let this world pass away. Hosanna to the God (Son) of David! If any one is holy, let him come; if any one is not so, let him repent. Maranatha. Amen.

Teaching of the Twelve Apostles

21. The Blessing

The Bishop when present, or the Priest, gives the blessing

The peace of God, which passeth all

understanding, keep your hearts and minds in the knowledge and love of God, and of his Son Jesus Christ our Lord; and the blessing of God Almighty, the Father, the Son, and the Holy Ghost, be amongst you, and remain with you always. Amen.

21. Commentary: This is the Trinitarian Blessing from Rite One [BCP 339]

22. Dismissal

The Deacon dismisses the people with these words

Go in Peace to love and serve the Lord.

People   Thanks be to God.

From the Easter Vigil through the Day of Pentecost "Alleluia, alleluia" may be added to any of the dismissals.

22. Commentary: The deacon dismisses as the one who is the real and symbolic representative of service to the community. He/she bids us go as the Body of Christ and act on what we have just heard and received. They are to lead and direct others into serving - to make sure that those who are powerless are not forgotten, such as the widows and the orphans [BCP 543]. The final rubric provides an option to add alleluias during the Easter season.

The Meaning and Symbols of Holy Eucharist

+

Wherefore with full assurance let us partake as of the Body and Blood of Christ: for in the figure of Bread is given to thee His Body, and in the figure of Wine His Blood; that thou by partaking of the Body and Blood of Christ, mayest be made of the same body and the same blood with Him. For thus we come to bear Christ in us, because His Body and Blood are distributed through our members; thus it is that, according to the blessed Peter, we become partakers of the divine nature.

Saint Cyril of Jerusalem – *Catechetical Lectires*

The Meaning and Symbols of Holy Eucharist

CHAPTER SIX

Devotions

"Everyone ought to examine themselves before they eat of the bread and drink from the cup. For those who eat and drink without discerning the body of Christ eat and drink judgment on themselves."

1 Corinthians 11:28, 29

Preparation for Holy Communion

I suspect you will find that as your appreciation for, and love of Christ in the Eucharist increases, so may your devotions. It is a sad commentary on the way we order our priorities that we give so little attention to preparing our hearts for worship. It is a common understanding among the clergy that the number of people in the church will double from the time we begin the processional (opening) hymn, to the offering of the Collect for Purity (the first prayer). And, we are always happy for the increase! Even so, for those who regularly enter late, you are missing out on the opportunity to abide in Christ prior to worship [John 15.1-17].

The Meaning and Symbols of Holy Eucharist

Jesus refers to his disciples as friends [John 15.15]. Friends enjoy one another's company – they look forward to spending time together. But Jesus is more than just our friend, he is also our Lord and Savior. This means he deserves our respect and honor, along with our love. Ideally preparation for Holy Eucharist will begin Saturday evening with Evening Prayer or private devotions, and resume during the quiet moments of Sunday morning.

When available, you ought to give yourself the blessing of making a confession: *All may; some should; none must.* Unfortunately, some Anglican clergy have not emphasized the importance of regular private confession. That practice is viewed by many parishioners as "too Roman Catholic". However, it is a spiritually healthy, and comforting biblical practice [James 5.13-16]. And, one of the most valuable ways to prepare for Holy Eucharist.

Prayers for Private Devotions

What follows is a form of preparation for Holy Eucharist, with additional prayers. Many of the prayers listed here are not included in the Book of Common Prayer (or Common Worship) found in the pew, so I have included a number of prayers from other supplementary prayer books for your use.

I urge you to consider the counsel of Father Lasance,

"The following prayers are so arranged as to occupy your time usefully whenever you assist at Mass in preparation for holy

communion. Remember, however, that you are not bound to say all these prayers; nor indeed any of them. In place of them, you may choose other prayers . . . If you can occupy a part or the whole of the time in meditating or reflecting on the Holy Eucharist in connection with the passion and death of Our Lord; on the Last Supper and the wonderful love and kindness of Jesus, our Savior, in instituting this marvelous sacrament; and in exciting in your heart holy desires and pious affections together with good resolutions, so much the better."

Rev. F.L. Lasance – *My Prayer-Book*

PREPARATION FOR HOLY COMMUNION

This first collection of prayers and guidelines comes from the 1950 edition of "The Practice of Religion – a Short Manual of Instructions and Devotions"

Anima Christi

Soul of Christ, sanctify me:
Body of Christ, save me:
Blood of Christ, refresh me:
Water from the side of Christ, wash me:
Passion of Christ, strengthen me:
O Good Jesu, hear me:
Within Thy wounds hide me:
Suffer me not to be separated from Thee:
From the malicious enemy defend me:
In the hour of my death call me,
And bid me come to Thee;

The Meaning and Symbols of Holy Eucharist

That with Thy Saints I may praise Thee
For all eternity. Amen.

Absolute Silence should be kept in the Nave and Sanctuary of the church for no less than 15 minutes prior to the processional hymn and the beginning of the Liturgy. This allows those who have come early to pray, to do so without distraction.

Ideally, preparation for Holy Communion also includes regular private confession.

It is well to be in Church a few minutes before the Service begins. Entering, genuflect if the Blessed Sacrament is there: if not, then bow to the Altar. Then kneel, sign the Cross and say silently:

In the Name + of the Father and of the Son and of the Holy Ghost. Amen.

Antiphon.   I will go unto the Altar of God.

PSALM XLIII. *Judica me, Deus.*

    1. Give sentence with me, O God, and defend my cause against the ungodly people; O deliver me from the deceitful and wicked man.
    2. For Thou art the God of my strength, why hast Thou put me from Thee? And why go I so heavily, while the enemy oppresseth me?
    3. O send out Thy light and Thy truth, that they may lead me, and bring me unto Thy holy hill, and to Thy dwelling;

The Meaning and Symbols of Holy Eucharist

    4. And that I may go unto the Altar of God, even unto the God of my joy and gladness, and upon the harp will I give thanks unto Thee, O God, my God.

    5. Why art thou so heavy, O my soul? And why art thou so disquieted within me?

    6. O put thy trust in God, for I will yet give Him thanks, which is the help of my countenance, and my God.

    Glory be to the Father, etc.

Antiphon: I will go unto the Altar of God, even unto the God of my joy and gladness.

Make me a clean heart, O Lord, and renew a right spirit within me. O grant me worthily to receive these Holy Mysteries and to love Thee with an everlasting love.

Before the Priest enters or while he is making his Preparation before the Altar, offer your Special Prayers and Thanksgivings, or your "Intentions" for the Mass, in your own words or as follows:

O Most Merciful Father, we humbly approach Thine Altar to offer and represent unto Thee the One, Pure, and Holy Sacrifice which Our Lord and Savior Jesus Christ made once upon the Cross and now ever pleads for us in Heaven and which He hath commanded us to show forth here on earth in this Memorial of His Death and Passion. Grant that this Offering may be acceptable at our hands, we beseech Thee, O God, and see us not as we are in ourselves but as we are in union with Our Savior Jesus Christ. We offer this Holy Eucharist unto Thee first for Thine Honour and Glory as the only Perfect Sacrifice which we can offer unto Thee. We also offer it in Thanksgiving for all Thy

The Meaning and Symbols of Holy Eucharist

Blessings (especially...), for the forgiveness of all our sins, (especially...), for the increase of all graces and virtues (especially...), for Thy Holy Church, for our Parish and for the Clergy (especially...), for those near and dear to us (especially...), for the sick (especially...), for the dying (especially...), for the faithful departed (especially...), and with all other holy intentions (especially...) which Thou wouldst have us make. All of which we ask through the Merits and Mediation of Jesus Christ, Our Lord and Redeemer. Amen.

Take away from us all our iniquities we beseech Thee O Lord; that with pure hearts and minds we may go unto Thine Altar, through Jesus Christ, Our Lord. Amen.

ADDITIONAL DEVOTIONS

Before Communion

Almighty and Everlasting God, behold I approach the Sacrament of Thine Only begotten Son, Jesus Christ. As one sick I come to the Physician of life: as unclean to the Fountain of Mercy: as blind to the Light of eternal splendour: as needy to the Lord of Heaven and earth: as naked to the King of Glory: a lost sheep to the Good Shepherd: a fallen creature to its Creator: desolate to the kind Comforter: miserable to the Pitier: guilty to the Bestower of pardon: sinful to the Justifier: hardened to the Giver of Grace.

The Meaning and Symbols of Holy Eucharist

I implore therefore the abundance of Thy Infinite Bounty that Thou wouldst vouchsafe to heal my sickness, to wash my foulness, to enlighten my darkness, to enrich my poverty, and to clothe my nackedness; that I may receive the Bread of Angels, the King of Kings, the Lord of Lords, with such reverence and humility, with such love and contrition, with such faith and devotion as is good for the welfare of my soul. Grant me, I pray, not only to receive the Sacrament of the Lord's Body and Blood of Thy Son Jesus Christ, that I may be incorporated in His Mystical Body and washed from every stain of sin. And O Most Loving Father, grant me that Him, Whom I now purpose to receive beneath a veil, I may hereafter behold with unveiled face, even Thy Beloved Son, Who with Thee and the Holy Ghost liveth and reigneth ever One God, for ever and ever. Amen. *(Adapted from Saint Thomas Aquinas.)*

Be Thou Merciful to me, O Good Jesus, and grant unto me, Thy poor suppliant, sometimes at least to feel in Holy Communion the cordial affection of Thy love, that my faith may grow stronger, my hope increase, my love enkindle …. O Most Holy and Loving Lord, Whom I now desire to receive with devotion, Thou knowest my weakness and how often I am weighed down, tempted, troubled, and defiled. To Thee I come for remedy. To thee I pray for comfort and help. Behold, I stand before Thee, beseeching Thy grace and imploring Thy mercy. O cheer Thy famishing suppliant, inkindle my coldness with the fire of Thy love, enlighten my blindness with the brightness of Thy Presence, and raise my heart unto Thee…. With the greatest devotion and burning love, with all the affection and fervour of my heart I desire to receive Thee, O Lord. O

The Meaning and Symbols of Holy Eucharist

deal with me in Thy mercy as Thou hast often dealt wonderfully with Thy saints of old, and prevent Thy servant in the blessing of Thy love, that I may worthily and devoutly approach and receive this Glorious Sacrament. Amen. *(Adapted from Saint Thomas 'a Kempis.)*

O Lord, we Thy servants bow down before Thy Holy Altar, waiting for the rich mercies which are from Thee. Send down upon us richly, we beseech Thee, Thy grace and benediction, and sanctify our souls and minds and bodies that we may worthily receive these Holy Mysteries, unto forgiveness of sins and everlasting life. For Thou, O God, with Thine Only-begotten Son and Thy Most Holy Spirit art to be worshiped and glorified now and for ever. *(Adapted from the Liturgy of Saint James.)*

O Lord, with this Holy Sacrifice we offer up our prayers and supplication unto Thee, asking for ourselves the peace from above, the Love of God, the Salvation of our Souls; for others that Thou wouldst be pleased to remember the poor, to help the suffering, to heal the sick, to comfort the broken-hearted, to watch over the traveler, to give peace to the Church, to grant prosperity to the world, bringing all people to love and confess Thee, the One and Only God. And especially do we pray for the heavenly and adorable gifts which are from Thee, and for the salvation of Thy priest who stands to offer them by Thy Divine Command. O Lord God, grant that our Oblations, hallowed by the Holy Ghost, may be well pleasing unto Thee, and accept them, we beseech Thee, for the forgiveness of our sins, the salvation of Thy people, and the repose of the faithful, that all at the Day of Judgment may find grace and mercy,

The Meaning and Symbols of Holy Eucharist

through Jesus Christ Our Lord.   *(Adapted from the Liturgy of Saint James.)*

Father, I have sinned against Heaven and before Thee, and am no more worthy to be called Thy son. I have ministered to my own desire and lusts, despising Thy Fatherly Love. I have dug for myself cisterns which hold no water, cisterns of earthly joys and vanities, leaving Thee the Fountain of many waters. I have sought pleasure in creatures which is only to be found Thee; and now behold all is vanity and vexation of spirit, for Thou hast made me for Thyself, and my heart findeth no true rest apart from Thee. Therefore I return to Thee, O Loving Father, Whose mercy is Infinite, Whose Goodness knoweth no end. Wherefore I cry, Father I have sinned against Heaven and before Thee and am no more worthy to be called Thy son; make me as one of Thine hired servants. O grant that henceforth I may walk in the straight path and narrow way that leadeth to Eternal Life, where with the Son and the Holy Spirit, Thou art unclouded Light and perfect Joy through Jesus Christ Our Lord. *(Adapted from Saint Augustine.)*

O Lord, Who dost bless those that bless Thee, and dost hallow those that put their trust in Thee, save Thy people and bless Thine inheritance. Guard, we beseech Thee, Thy Holy Church. Hallow those that love the beauty of Thine House. Forsake not us who put our trust in Thee. Give peace to the world, to the Church, to the Priesthood, to our Rulers, and to all Thy people; for every good gift and every perfect work is from above, coming from Thee, the Father of Lights, to Whom we ascribe, with the Son and the Holy Ghost, all glory, thanksgiving and worship now ever, unto

The Meaning and Symbols of Holy Eucharist

the ages of ages. *(Adapted from the Liturgy of Saint Chrysostom.)*

O Lord, we offer unto Thee with this Holy Sacrifice ourselves and souls and bodies for Thee to accept for the sake of Thy Beloved Son, Jesus Christ, Our Lord. Grant, O God that hallowed by our union with Him, and cleansed in His Precious Blood, we may be an acceptable offering in Thy sight, and may evermore give our selves up in loving service and holy obedience to Thee; Who art to be praised and glorified, One God, for ever and ever.

O Lord, by this Most Sacred Mystery of Thy Body and Blood, grant us Thy manifold Gifts of Grace ... that we may receive this Blessed Sacrament to our health and comfort. For Thou hast said, "The Bread which I give is My Flesh for the life of the world. I am the Living Bread which came down from Heaven. If any man eat of this Bread, he shall live for ever." ... O Bread most sweet that ever refreshest and never failest, may we feed upon thee and may our inmost soul be filled with Thine Heavenly Peace. May we in our pilgrimage so receive Thee that we may not faint upon our way, but come in safety to the end of our journey. O Holy Bread, O Living Bread, O Adorable Bread, the very Body and Blood of Our Savior Christ, come unto us and cleanse us from all defilement of flesh and spirit. Drive away from us all our foes and so preserve us that we may come in safety to Thine Heavenly Kingdom, no longer to see Thee in Holy Mysteries, but then face to face. *(Taken from Prayers variously ascribed to Saints Anselm and Ambrose.)*

O Lord, as we receive Thy Precious Body and Blood, send

forth Thine unseen Hand which is full of blessings and bountifully bless us all. Have mercy upon us and strengthen us by Thy Divine Power. Take away from us the sinful working of all fleshly lusts. Drive from before our eyes the encompassing gloom of sin and unite us with the blessed company of all faithful people, who have been well pleasing unto Thee. For through Thee and with Thee and in Thee, with the Father and Holy Ghost be all praise, honour, might, majesty, dominion and power, now and for ever, unto the ages of ages. Amen. *(Adapted from the Liturgy of Saint Mark.)*

We beseech Thee, O Lord, that this Holy Communion may be unto us a guide and provision for our journey unto the haven of everlasting Salvation. May it be to us comfort in sorrow, strength in trial, patience in difficulty, medicine in sickness, delight in prosperity, and love in all things. By these most Holy Mysteries, which we would receive, grant us right faith, firm hope, and perfect charity, purification of desire, gladness of mind, ardent love of Thee, and a due remembrance of the Passion of Thy Beloved Son, with grace to keep our lives full of faith and virtue. And in the hour of our departure grant that we may receive this great Mystery with true faith, sure hope, and sincere charity unto Everlasting Life. Amen. *(Adapted from Old Sarum Rite.)*

After Communion

Almighty and Everlasting God, Preserver of Souls and Redeemer of the world, most graciously regard me Thy servant prostrate before Thy Majesty; and this Sacrifice

The Meaning and Symbols of Holy Eucharist

which in honour of Thy Name we have presented before Thee, for the Salvation of the faithful, whether living or departed and also for our sins and offences do Thou most mercifully regard. Take away from me Thy wrath, grant me Thy grace and mercy, open to me the door of Paradise, mightily rescue me from all evil and forgive whatever sin of my own guilt I have committed. And make me so to persevere in Thy Commandments in this world, that I may be made worthy to be united to the flock of the Elect, through Thy Bounty, O my God, Whose Blessed Name and Hour and Kingdom remaineth forever and ever. Amen. *(Adapted from Old Sarum Rite.)*

Almighty and Everlasting God, Jesus Christ my Lord, be Thou merciful to my sins, through the reception of Thy Body and Blood. For Thou, O Lord, hast said "Whoso eateth My Flesh and drinketh My Blood dwelleth in Me and I in Him." Wherefore I humbly beseech Thee, that Thou wouldst create in me a pure heart, and renew a right spirit within me; that Thou wouldst deign to stablish me with Thy Firm Spirit; and so deliver me from the snares of the devil and from all my sins, that I may attain to be a partaker of Thine heavenly joys; Who livest and reignest with the Father and the Holy Ghost, one God, for ever and ever. Amen. *(Adapted from Old Sarum Rite.)*

We yield Thee thanks, O Lord, Holy Father, Almighty, Everlasting God, Who not for any merit of ours, but of Thy mercy only, hast been pleased to feed us sinners, Thine unworthy servants, with the Precious Body and Blood of Thy Son, Our Lord, Jesus Christ. And we beseech Thee, that this Holy Communion may not accuse us unto

The Meaning and Symbols of Holy Eucharist

condemnation but may be to us pardon and salvation. Let it be to us an armour of faith and a shield of good resolution. Let is be to us the riddance of all vices, the killing of all evil desires and longings, and the increase of love and patience, of humility and obedience, and of all virtues; a firm defense against all enemies visible and invisible, a constraining power to purity and holiness. Let it make us always cling closely to Thee, the One, True, and Only God, and end our earthy days in peace. And we pray Thee to bring us to that Heavenly Banquet, where Thou with Thy Son and the Holy Ghost art to Thy Saints true light, everlasting joy, and perfect happiness. Amen. *(Adapted from Old Sarum Rite.)*

May the performance of our bounden duty be pleasing unto Thee, O God, and grant that this Holy Sacrifice which we, though unworthy, have presented before Thy Divine Majesty, may be acceptable unto Thee and obtain mercy for us and for those for whom we pray, by Thy compassion, Who livest and reignest One God, world, without end. Amen. *(Adapted from Old Sarum Rite.)*

O Lord, we would remember in our prayers the Holy Catholic Church, that Thou mayst graciously vouchsafe to increase it in faith, hope and charity. We would remember the sick and suffering, the desolate and sorrowful, the poor and destitute, that Thou mayst heal, comfort and relieve them. We would remember the souls of the faithful departed, that they may rest in peace where their works do follow them. Mercifully perform this, we beseech Thee, O Eternal and Almighty Father, to Whom we offer this Holy Sacrifice. Amen. *(Adapted from the Mozarabic Liturgy.)*

The Meaning and Symbols of Holy Eucharist

Most Blessed Lord and Savior Jesus Christ the great High Priest, Who for us didst offer Thyself upon the Cross, a pure and spotless Victim, and didst ordain this Holy Mystery and give us Thy Flesh to eat and Thy Blood to drink, saying, Do this in remembrance of Me, I pray Thee to wash us from our sins, and teach us by Thy Holy Spirit to receive these Sacred Gifts with such reverence and honour, such devotion and love as is meet and fitting. Make us through Thy Grace, always to believe and think and speak of this great Mystery as shall please Thee and be good for our souls. Let Thy Holy Spirit enter into our hearts and speak and teach all truth. For these Sacred Mysteries are beyond man's understanding. In Thy Mercy grant us to receive this Holy Eucharist with a clean heart and pure mind. Drive away all vain, evil, impure and unholy thoughts. Defend us with the loving and faithful protection of the blessed angels, and keep us free from the spirit of pride and vanity, envy and blasphemy, doubt and distrust and fill us with boundless love of Thee. Amen. *(From Prayers ascribed to Saint Anselm or Saint Ambrose.)*

O Most Merciful Savior, look with compassion, we beseech Thee, upon us who have received the sacred gifts of Thy Body and Blood. Bless the lips which have praised Thee, the heart which has loved Thee, the body which has worshipped Thee, the soul which has adored Thee, that in the world to come they may be Thine for ever. Amen.

O God, Who art Holy and Wonderful and Mighty, Whose Power and Wisdom have no end, before Whom all things bow, and the heavens and earth declare Thy Glory, grant me to love Thee and to worship Thee for ever and ever.

The Meaning and Symbols of Holy Eucharist

Guide me unto the perfect light, that, illumined by its radiance, all darkness may flee away. Let the holy flame of Thy love so burn in my heart that it may be made pure and holy, for none but the pure in heart can see and know an receive Thee, the King of Kings, Our Lord and God. Amen. *(Adapted from Saint Augustine.)*

May Our Lord and Savior, Jesus Christ, Who comes to us in the Blessed Sacrament of the Altar, be to us the Way to Everlasting life.

In the Peace of Christ let us depart.

In the Peace of Christ let us sing.

From Glory to Glory let us go forth, hymning in our hearts to Thee, the Savior of our souls. Glory be to the Father and to the Son and to the Holy Ghost. We praise Thee the Savior of our Souls.

From Strength to Strength advancing, we who have accomplished the Divine Ministration in Thy Temple, now pray unto Thee, O God. Vouchsafe to us Thy Mercy, guide our feet aright, root us firmly in Thy love, and at last count us worthy of Thine Heavenly Kingdom, through the Merits and Mediation of Thy Son, to Whom with Thee and the Holy Ghost be Glory, Honour, and Power unto the Ages of Ages. *(Adapted from the Liturgy of Saint James.)*

The Meaning and Symbols of Holy Eucharist

Lord, you now have set your servant free, To go in peace, as you have promised; For these eyes of mine have seen the Savior, Whom you have prepared, for all the world to see: A light to enlighten the nations, And the glory of your people Israel. Glory to Father, and to the Son and To the Holy Spirit, as it was in the beginning is now and will be forever. Amen *(The Song of Simeon, Luke 2:29-32 – from the Book of Common Prayer (1979), pg. 120)*

The Meaning and Symbols of Holy Eucharist

RECOMMENDED PSALTER & SCRIPTURE READINGS

Consider reading through a passage of Scripture for your devotions, and offering it as a prayer. Here are some suggestions:

Psalm 51, 84, 85, 86, 116:10-16, 130

Genesis 22.1-19
Exodus 12.1-27
Leviticus 16
Hosea 6.6
Matthew 26.17-29
Mark 14.12-25
Luke 22.7-20, 24.13-35
John 1.36, 6.25-65
Acts 2.42
1 Corinthians 10:16-17; 11:23-32
Hebrews 6.19-20, and chapters 7, 8, 9 and 10.1-25
Revelation chapters 4 and 5

The Meaning and Symbols of Holy Eucharist

Additional Prayers

Most of the following prayers come from the 1979 Book of Common Prayer.

PRIVATE PRAYERS BEFORE HOLY EUCHARIST

A Collect for Saturdays
Almighty God, who after the creation of the world rested from all your works and sanctified a day of rest for all your creatures: Grant that we, putting away all earthly anxieties, may be duly prepared for the service of your sanctuary, and that our rest here upon earth may be a preparation for the eternal rest promised to your people in heaven; through Jesus Christ our Lord. **Amen.**

A Collect for the Presence of Christ *(Saturday Evening)*
Lord Jesus, stay with us, for evening is at hand and the day is past; be our companion in the way, kindle our hearts, and awaken hope, that we may know you as you are revealed in Scripture and the breaking of bread. Grant this for the sake of your love. **Amen.**

For Protection
Assist us mercifully, O Lord, in these our supplications and prayers, and dispose the way of thy servants towards the attainment of everlasting salvation; that, among all the changes and chances of this mortal life, they may ever be defended by thy gracious and ready help; through Jesus Christ our Lord. **Amen.**

The Meaning and Symbols of Holy Eucharist

A Prayer of Self-Dedication
Almighty and eternal God, so draw our hearts to thee, so guide our minds, so fill our imaginations, so control our wills, that we may be wholly thine, utterly dedicated unto thee; and then use us, we pray thee, as thou wilt, and always to thy glory and the welfare of thy people; through our Lord and Savior Jesus Christ. **Amen.**

By Thomas Cranmer
Blessed Lord, who caused all holy Scriptures to be written for our learning: Grant us so to hear them, read, mark, learn, and inwardly digest them, that we may embrace and ever hold fast the blessed hope of everlasting life, which you have given us in our Savior Jesus Christ; who lives and reigns with you and the Holy Spirit, one God, for ever and ever. **Amen.**

By Thomas Cranmer
Almighty God, give us grace to cast away the works of darkness, and put on the armor of light, now in the time of this mortal life in which your Son Jesus Christ came to visit us in great humility; that in the last day, when he shall come again in his glorious majesty to judge both the living and the dead, we may rise to the life immortal; through him who lives and reigns with you and the Holy Spirit, one God, now and for ever. **Amen.**

Devotion
O Lord Jesus Christ, Son of the living God, Who, by the will of the Father, with the cooperation of the Holy Spirit, have by Your death given life to the world, deliver me by this Your Most Sacred Body and Blood from all my sins and

from every evil. Make me always cling to Your commandments, and never permit me to be separated from You. Who with the same God the Father and the Holy Spirit, live and reign, God, world without end. **Amen.**

Devotion
O Lord Jesus Christ, Who said to Your Apostles: "Peace I leave with you, My peace I give to you," regard not my sins but the faith of Your Church, and deign to give her peace and unity according to Your Will: Who live and reign, God, world without end. **Amen.**

Devotion
Let not the partaking of Your Body, O Lord Jesus Christ, which I, though unworthy, presume to receive, turn to my judgment and condemnation; but through Your goodness, may it become a safeguard and an effective remedy, both of soul and body. Who live and reign with God the Father, in the unity of the Holy Spirit, God, world without end. **Amen.**

PRIVATE PRAYERS AFTER HOLY COMMUNION

A Collect for Sundays
O God, you make us glad with the weekly remembrance of the glorious resurrection of your Son our Lord: Give us this day such blessing through our worship of you, that the week to come may be spent in your favor; through Jesus Christ our Lord. **Amen.**

The Meaning and Symbols of Holy Eucharist

A Collect for Sundays
Lord God, whose Son our Savior Jesus Christ triumphed over the powers of death and prepared for us our place in the new Jerusalem: Grant that we, who have this day given thanks for his resurrection, may praise you in that City of which he is the light, and where he lives and reigns for ever and ever. **Amen.**

Devotion
What has passed our lips as food, O Lord, may we possess in purity of heart, that what is given to us in time, be our healing for eternity. May Your Body, O Lord, which I have eaten, and Your Blood which I have drunk, cleave to my very soul, and grant that no trace of sin be found in me, whom these pure and holy mysteries have renewed. Who live and reign, world without end. **Amen.**

Devotion
We humbly beseech You, almighty God, to grant that those whom You refresh with Your sacraments, may serve you worthily by a life well pleasing to You. Through our Lord Jesus Christ, Your Son, Who lives and reigns, world without end. **Amen.**

Prayer of St. Thomas Aquinas
I render thanks to Thee, O Lord, Holy Father, Everlasting God, who hast vouchsafed, not for any merits of mine, but of Thy great mercy only, to feed me a great sinner, Thine unworthy servant, with the precious Body and Blood of Thy Son, our Lord Jesus Christ ; and I pray that this Holy Communion may not be for my judgment and condemnation, but for my pardon and salvation. Let it be

unto me an armor of faith and a shield of good purpose, a riddance of all vices, and a rooting out of all evil desires ; an increase of love and patience, of humility and obedience, and of all virtues ; a firm defense against the wiles of all my enemies, visible and invisible ; a perfect quieting of all my impulses, fleshy and spiritual ; a cleaving unto Thee, the one true God ; and a blessed consummation of my end when Thou dost call. And I pray that Thou wouldst vouchsafe to bring me a sinner to that unspeakable Feast where Thou, with Thy Son and Thy Holy Spirit, art to Thy holy ones true light, full blessedness, everlasting joy, and perfect happiness Through the same Christ our Lord. **Amen.**

Prayer of St. Bonaventure
O most sweet Lord Jesus Christ, transfix the affections of my inmost soul with that most joyous and healthful wound of Thy love, with true, serene, holiest Apostolic charity, that my soul may ever languish and melt with genuine love and longing for Thee, that it may desire Thee, and faint for Thy courts, long to be dissolved and to be with Thee. Grant that my soul may hunger after Thee, the Bread of Angels, the Refreshment of holy souls, our daily and supersubstantial Bread, who hast all sweetness and savor, and the sweetness of every taste. Let my heart ever hunger after and feed upon Thee, upon whom the Angels desire to look, and my inmost soul be filled with the sweetness of Thy savor. May it ever thirst for Thee, the Fountain of life, the Source of wisdom and knowledge, the Fountain of eternal light, the Torrent of pleasure, the Richness of the House of God. May it ever yearn for Thee, seek Thee, find Thee, stretch towards Thee, attain to Thee, meditate upon Thee, speak of Thee,

The Meaning and Symbols of Holy Eucharist

and do all things to the praise and glory of Thy holy name, with humility and discretion, with love and delight, with readiness and affection, with perseverance even unto the end. And be Thou ever my hope and my whole confidence ; my riches ; my delight, my pleasure, and my joy ; my rest and tranquility ; my peace, my sweetness and my fragrance ; my sweet savor, my food and refreshment ; my refuge and my help ; my wisdom ; my portion, my possession, and my treasure, in whom my mind and my heart may ever remain fixed and firm, and rooted immovably, henceforth and forevermore. **Amen.**

Private Prayers offered by the Celebrant

In a very traditional or "Anglo-catholic" Mass, you may notice the celebrant saying prayers quietly to himself. While those private prayers are not precisely the same from celebrant to celebrant, the following rubrics and prayers will provide you with a good inside glimpse into what is being said. These excerpts are from the Private Prayers at the Mass in The English Missal, 1958.

After the Offertory,

Which having been said, if the Mass be solemn, the Deacon presents the Paten with the Host to the celebrant: if it be private, the Priest himself takes the Paten with the Host, which he offers saying:

Receive, O holy Father, almighty everlasting God, this spotless host, which I, thine unworthy servant, offer unto thee, my living and true God, for my numberless sins, offences, and negligences, and for all who stand here around, as also for all faithful christians, both living and departed: that to me and to them it may avail for salvation unto life eternal.   Amen.

Then making a cross with the same Paten, he places the Host upon the Corporal. The deacon ministers the wine, the Subdeacon the water in the Chalice: or if it be a private Mass, the Priest pours in both, and blesses with the sign of the Cross the water to be mixed in the Chalice, saying:

The Meaning and Symbols of Holy Eucharist

O God, who didst wondrously create, and yet more wondrously renew the dignity of human nature: grant that by the mystery of this water and wine we may be made co-heirs of his divinity, who vouchsafed to be made partaker of our humanity, even Jesus Christ thy Son our Lord: Who liveth and reigneth with thee in the unity of the Holy Ghost, one God: World without end. Amen

In Masses of the Dead the foregoing Prayer is said: but the water is not blessed.

Then he receives the Chalice, and offers it, saying:

We offer unto thee, O Lord, the cup of salvation, humbly beseeching thy mercy: that in the sight of thy divine majesty it may ascend as a sweet-smelling savour for our salvation, and for that of the whole world. Amen.

Then he makes the sign of the cross with the chalice, and places it upon the Corporal, and covers it with the Pall: then with hands joined upon the Altar, he says, bowing slightly:

In a humble spirit, and with a contrite heart, may we be accepted of thee, O Lord: and so let our sacrifice be offered in thy sight this day, that it may be pleasing unto thee, O Lord God.

The Meaning and Symbols of Holy Eucharist

Standing erect, he extends his hands, raises them and joins them, and lifting his eyes to heaven and straight way lowering them, he says:

Come, O thou Fount of holiness, almighty, eternal God: *He blesses the Oblations, proceeding*: and bl+ess this sacrifice, made ready for thy holy name.

For the ablutions, the Missal cites Psalm 26:6-12, concluding with the Gloria Patri.

Private prayers after the Fraction:

He puts the particle into the Chalice, saying secretly:

May this mingling and hallowing of the Body and Blood of our Lord Jesus Christ avail us who receive it unto everlasting life. Amen.

He covers the Chalice, genuflects, rises, and bowing to the Sacrament, joins his hands, and beating his breast thrice, says in an audible voice: the Agnus Dei.

Then bowing, with hands joined upon the Altar, he says secretly the following Prayers:

O Lord Jesu Christ, who saidst to thine Apostles, Peace I leave with you, my peace I give unto you: regard not my [our] sins, but the faith of thy Church: and vouchsafe to

The Meaning and Symbols of Holy Eucharist

grant her peace and unity according to thy will: Who liveth and reignest God, throughout all ages; world without end. Amen.

Then turning to the People with the host, the Celebrant says:

Behold the Lamb of God, behold Him that taketh away the sin of the world.

He genuflects, rises, and says:

I will receive the bread of heaven, and call upon the name of the Lord.

Then bowing slightly, he takes both parts of the Host between the thumb and forefinger of his left hand, and places the Paten between the same forefinger and the middle finger, and beating his breast three times with his right hand he says thrice, devoutly and humbly, raising his voice a little:

Lord, I am not worthy, *And he proceeds secretly:* that thou should enter under my roof: but speak the word only, and my soul shall be healed.

Afterwards signing himself with his right hand with the Host over the Paten he says:

The Body of our Lord Jesus Christ preserve my soul unto everlasting life. Amen.

The Meaning and Symbols of Holy Eucharist

And bowing himself, he reverently takes both parts of the Host: which having been consumed, he puts the Paten down upon the Corporal, and raising himself, joins his hands, and is still for a little space in meditation on the Most Holy Sacrament. Then he uncovers the Chalice, genuflects, collects the fragments, if there be any, and cleanses the Paten over the Chalice, saying meanwhile:

What reward shall I give unto the Lord for all the benefits that hath done unto me? I will receive the cup of salvation, and call upon the name of the Lord. I will call upon the Lord which is worthy to be praised, so shall I be safe from mine enemies.

He takes the Chalice in his right hand and signing himself with, says:

The Blood of our Lord Jesus Christ preserve my soul unto everlasting life. Amen.

Holding the Paten under the Chalice with his left hand, he reverently receives the Blood with the particle. Having received it, if there be any communicated, let him communicate them, before he purify himself.

After Communication

Afterward he says:

Grant, O Lord, that what we have taken with our mouths we may receive in purity of heart: and let this temporal gift avail for our healing unto life eternal.

Meanwhile he presents the Chalice to the minister, who pours into it a little wine, wherewith he purifies himself: then he continues:

Let thy Body, O Lord, which I have taken, and thy Blood which I have drunk, cleave unto my members: and grant; that no stain of sin may remain in me, whom thou hast refreshed with these pure and holy sacraments: Who livest and reignest world without end. Amen.

He washes and wipes his fingers, and takes the ablution: he wipes his mouth and the Chalice, which, having folded the Corporal, he covers and places on the Altar as before: then he proceeds with the Mass.

The Post-Communion Prayer

The post-communion prayer is said, followed by the dismissal.

Having said Ite, Missa est, *or* Let us bless the Lord, *the Priest bows himself before the midst of the Altar, and with hands joined thereon, says secretly:*

The Meaning and Symbols of Holy Eucharist

Let this my bounden duty and service be pleasing to thee, O Holy Trinity: and grant; that the sacrifice, which I unworthy, have offered before the eyes of thy majesty, may be acceptable to thee, and may through thy mercy obtain thy gracious favour for me and all for whom I have offered it. Through Christ our Lord. Amen.

Then he kisses the Altar: and raising his eyes, extending, raising, and joining his hands, and bowing his head to the Cross he says: May God almighty, *and turning to the people, blessing them only once, even in solemn Masses, he proceeds:* the Father, the + Son and the Holy Ghost, bless you. R. Amen."

Only a Pontifical Mass has a three-fold blessing.

As the Priest is leaving he repeats silently to himself John 1:1-14.

+

The Meaning and Symbols of Holy Eucharist

CHAPTER SEVEN

Anglican Identity

The pearl of eternity is the church, or temple of God within thee, the consecrated place of divine worship where alone thou canst worship God in spirit and truth.

– William Law

Anglicans seem to have a confused identity, even among themselves. We hear questions like: Are you Catholic? Do you have a pope? Are you Protestant? Weren't you founded by King Henry the VIIIth? These questions are not always easy to answer due to the fact that we are historically both Protestant and Catholic. To add to the confusion, a number of Anglicans are divided on what period of history they hold to as their origin. Some Anglicans see themselves as products of the Reformation Movement, and others primarily identify themselves with the Church Fathers and the Early Church.

The following questions are answered here from the perspective that the Anglican Church finds her origins in the Early Church. It was in the midst of the Reformation Movement (1500s) and again later during the Oxford Movement (1800s) that the writings of the Early Church were re-discovered and shaped the form of Anglican catholicism that we enjoy today.

The Meaning and Symbols of Holy Eucharist

Frequently Asked Questions about Anglicanism

In your hearts set apart Christ as Lord. Always be prepared to give an answer to everyone who asks you to give a reason for the hope that you have. But do this with gentleness and respect . . .
    Saint Peter

It should be noted that not all Anglicans would find agreement with the answers presented here, and these responses are not presented as the official dogma of the Anglican Communion. Rather, they are the answers that you would receive if you asked them of this particular parish priest.

Who are Anglicans?

Anglicans are the third largest group of Catholic Christians in the world, numbering around 80 million people. The two largest groups of Catholic-Christians are the Roman Catholics, and the Eastern Orthodox. Prior to the Great Schism of AD1054 when the Eastern Church (Orthodox) and Western Church (Latin) divided, the Christian Church was united without denominations. A core value for Anglicans is to practice Christianity as did the early unbroken Church, with the hope that we may some day be re-united. Finally, the most important aspect of our identity is that we are followers of Jesus.

The Meaning and Symbols of Holy Eucharist

Are Anglicans Catholics?

Yes, we are Catholics, but we are not "Roman Catholics." The word "catholic" actually means "universal", but it is also used to identify Christians who recognize an unbroken line of people from Jesus' first followers to the present, who were anointed by the Holy Spirit for ministry. This heritage is called "apostolic succession" and Anglicans share that lineage with Roman Catholics and Eastern Orthodox Christians. Historically, Christians lived and worshipped in Britain during the earliest years of the Church during the Roman Empire. Celtic Christianity continued as a distinct expression of the Catholic Faith for many centuries. Anglicans (Christians from the Church of England) came to North America as pilgrims, pioneers and residents of the first colonies.

Do Anglicans have a pope?

No. The early undivided Catholic Church made decisions through councils where bishops and others met to seek God's direction over matters of faith, through prayer and debate. For example, the Nicene Creed and the Definition of Chalcedon, which have defined Trinitarian doctrine and the nature of Christ for nearly 1700 years, were the products of Church Councils. During those early centuries the Bishop of Rome was known as "the first among equals" - certainly someone who deserved much respect, but still only a bishop among fellow bishops. Prior to the Great Schism of 1054, the Emperor called the early Ecumenical Councils together and presided over them. The Emperor sought the advice of the Bishop of Rome, who in turn presided over lesser councils and synods to resolve theological and ecclesiastical issues. It is noteworthy that the Bishop of Rome (the Pope) did not have broad unilateral authority during the early centuries of the Church. Anglicanism follows a similar pattern, where an archbishop will preside over councils, but he is still simply a bishop among a college of bishops. The archbishop's authority allows him to call the College of Bishops together, to introduce an agenda, and to preside over the meetings, but he does not have unilateral authority to introduce or revise matters of Faith and Doctrine.

Do Anglicans have a hierarchy like the Roman Catholic Church?

Anglicans only recognize the Biblical and Early Church hierarchy as authoritative: bishops, presbyters and deacons. The bishop of a diocese has the final word for that diocese. For the sake of collegiality, communication and global mission, American Anglican dioceses have voluntarily aligned with archbishops, other dioceses and national churches. [See above.]

May Anglican priests marry?

Yes. Saint Paul recommended that ministers such as himself refrain from marriage, if possible. [1 Corinthians 7:8] But the Church does not forbid the clergy to marry.

Do Anglicans have monks and nuns?

Yes, but not many. Henry VIII closed down the monasteries and convents during his reign, and they have never recovered from that loss.

Are Anglicans Protestant?

Yes and no. Anglicans were among those who protested

the abuses of the Roman Catholic Church during the Reformation Movement of the 1500s and later. However, none of the Christian denominations are now what they were in the 1500s. So, the label "Protestant" is not very helpful. Since then, "Protestant" has come to mean "churches that are not Catholic" because few Christian denominations are still protesting the Roman Catholic Church. So, if by "Protestant" one means "not Catholic" then Anglicans are not really Protestants. At least, certainly not in the way other denominations are Protestant. The difference between Anglicans and Protestants is most apparent by the fact that Anglicans were the only group of protesting Christians within the Reformation Movement who maintained the ancient Catholic Liturgy and continued the ministration of the seven Sacraments. As you can imagine, the "Protestant" label and the "Catholic" label carry a variety of implications depending on the context.

Wasn't the Church of England established by King Henry the VIII?

The Catholic Church in England began a reformation process during the reign of Henry the VIII in the 1500s. During that time Henry used the Church to further his own political agenda. Henry did much harm to the Church during his reign, so he is no hero to Anglicans. However, some church leaders of the time used Henry's self-centered distractions as an opportunity to eliminate some of the problems that had developed in the medieval Catholic Church, and rolled back the beliefs and practices to an earlier age when the Church was a united Catholic Church, before the Western and Eastern Church divided. Many suffered and died to make that a reality. To diminish the sacrifice of those English martyrs by attributing their faith to the political whims of King Henry is a travesty. The fact that Anglicanism has no such visible founder as Luther, Calvin or Knox is a testimony to the desire of the Anglican reformers to restore the doctrine and practices of the Early Church in England. This is why you will find no Anglican Creed. Our only Doctrine is Holy Scripture. Our only Creeds are the Apostles' Creed and the Nicene Creed.

What do Anglicans believe?

We believe that the Bible is the revealed Word of God, and that it is our primary source for truth, for knowing God and understanding His purposes. That truth is summarized for us in the Apostles' Creed and the Nicene Creed. These two creeds outline the Christian Faith as Trinitarian (God the Father, God the Son, and God the Holy Spirit; three in one), and they affirm the divinity and humanity of Jesus Christ. We believe that faith in Jesus Christ as our Lord and Savior is necessary for salvation. Salvation is that state of being where we are in union with God and adopted as His people.

Do Anglicans believe the Bible is the Word of God?

Yes. [See above.]

How do Anglicans worship?

We continue to worship as the earliest Christians worshipped from 2,000 years ago to the present, by celebrating Holy Eucharist, (also known as the Great Thanksgiving, the Lord's Supper, and Holy Communion).

The Meaning and Symbols of Holy Eucharist

This includes praying, singing, reading Scripture, hearing the Gospel, preaching, declaring the Creed, celebrating and sharing Communion. We worship to glorify God, not to entertain one another.

Are Anglicans "Born Again" Christians?
Yes! "Born Again" refers to the fact that we have died to our broken nature and have been re-born with a new nature in Christ.

Who are Christians?
"Christian" literally means "Christ-like" and refers to the people who are following Jesus Christ. Unfortunately, we don't always follow Jesus as well as we ought to, but that is our goal.

Are there hypocrites in your church?
Yes, we all are! God said that we all fall short of perfection – everyone has – even you. [Romans 3.23] That is why we need to come together as people earnestly seeking forgiveness. Jesus said, "blessed are the merciful, for they shall receive mercy."

Do Anglicans believe in the Sacraments?
We believe in the two sacraments ordered by Christ: Baptism and Holy Communion. And we practice the five pastoral sacraments established by the Church to convey and affirm grace and healing to her members: Confirmation, Marriage, Reconciliation, Ordination and Unction.

Do Anglicans pray to Mary and the Saints?
Anglicans believe that Mary and the Saints are praying for

the Church even more now than they did before they died. We believe that the saints have more insight and a greater passion for the Church now than they did when they lived on earth. Therefore some Anglicans ask for their prayers now, just as they might ask any christian to pray with them or for them. However, Anglicans are not required to pray to Mary or to pray the rosary.

Are Anglicans Pro-Life?

Yes. We believe that it is self-evident that an unborn child deserves as much respect and protection as those of us who already were given birth.

Why do you call the pastor "Father"?

One of the most common and challenging questions from Christians of other traditions is combined with a reminder or recitation of Matthew 23.9. That verse is included with those surrounding it, here:

> *But you are not to be called rabbi, for you have one teacher, and you are all brothers. And call no man your father on earth, for you have one Father, who is in heaven. Neither be called instructors, for you have one instructor, the Christ. The greatest among you shall be your servant. Whoever exalts himself will be humbled, and whoever humbles himself will be exalted.* Matthew 23.8-12 (ESV)

The *Call No Man Father* Question:

One day while sitting on a park bench and wearing my priest collar, a man came passing by and without pausing in his stride, he turned toward me and smiled knowingly and said "Call no man father!" continuing on without

The Meaning and Symbols of Holy Eucharist

waiting for a reply. To be honest, I don't recall whether I replied or not – at least in my imagination, I retorted "Call no man teacher!"

As one who grew up in a fundamentalist denomination, I completely understand where that man was coming from in his gentle condemnation. I was raised with the understanding that Jesus' admonition in Matthew 23 was directed at Roman Catholic priests. And even though that is no longer my understanding, I still greatly respect the desire of any Christian to faithfully obey Christ. So, if you are uncomfortable using the title "father", don't use it! It is more important that you follow your conscience regarding your understanding of God's Word, rather than use a title. Personally, I am not offended when simply addressed by my first name. The title that I don't care for is "reverend." As I read Matthew's text, within our culture, the title "reverend" fits the context of Jesus' admonition in Matthew 23 more so than does the term "father".

The word "reverend" etymologically refers to one who is revered, or who is worthy of reverence, or respect. The term originated in the late 15th century when clergy were often, not only revered, but also feared. It is rewarding to be respected, but only God should be revered. Over the years the term "reverend" has come to be used as a formal title designating a clergy person, and I use it as such in formal correspondence for the sake of communication, but I don't really like it.

The pride of wishing to be revered above other men is the very problem that Jesus addressed to the crowds and disciples regarding the scribes and Pharisees in Matthew 23. To understand Jesus' warning to call no one "my master" (Rabbi), "teacher" or "father", we must consider the context of the passage. In Matthew 23.2, Jesus recognized that the scribes and Pharisees had authority because they represented Moses, "so practice and observe whatever they tell you." But Jesus warned the people not to practice what the scribes and Pharisees do, because of their pride and hypocrisy. The problem then isn't so much with the title but the reason why the religious leaders wanted the title and position, and how they administered the authority associated with it: they viewed themselves as superior to other people in their social status, and their ability to understand, administer and keep God's Law.

Moses identified the same issue when he warned future kings not to think of themselves as better than their subjects; rather to be devoted to studying God's Law [Deuteronomy 17:20a].

Jesus dealt with the sin of pride of place among the disciples when they argued over who was the greatest [Mark 9.33-37], and later when James and John tried to secure a place of honor in Jesus' kingdom [Mark 10.35-45.] "Whoever would be first among you" Jesus said, "must be slave of all."

The sins that Jesus warns against in Matthew 23.8-12 are pride and arrogance.

Paul, an exemplary rabbinical student [Acts 22.3] who was well aware of the pride of the religious leaders, used the word "father" to indicate that he was as a spiritual father of those he taught and mentored:

> *I do not write these things to make you ashamed, but to admonish you as my beloved children. For though you have countless guides in Christ, you do not have many fathers. For I became your father in Christ Jesus through the gospel. I urge you, then, be imitators of me. That is why I sent you Timothy, my beloved and faithful child in the Lord, to remind you of my ways in Christ, as I teach them everywhere in every church.* 1 Corinthians 4:14-17 (ESV)

Regarding Timothy, Paul wrote:

> *But you know Timothy's proven worth, how as a son with a father he has served me in the gospel.*
> Philippians 2.22 (ESV)

[For more examples, see also 2 Kings 2.12; Acts 7.2; Romans 4:16; 1 Thessalonians. 2.11; 1 Timothy 1.2; 5.1-2, and Philemon 10]

Clearly, Paul viewed the Church as a family, and used those terms to describe her members.

I included the full context of Jesus' admonishment against pride in Matthew 23, because he names other titles/positions besides "father". Jesus also included "rabbi", "teacher" and "instructor" (depending on the English translation).

Paul was not adverse to using the title "teacher" in the context of ministry:

The Meaning and Symbols of Holy Eucharist

And God has appointed in the church first apostles, second prophets, third teachers, then miracles, then gifts of healing, helping, administrating, and various kinds of tongues.
1 Corinthians 12:28 (ESV)

And he gave the apostles, the prophets, the evangelists, the shepherds and teachers, to equip the saints for the work of ministry, for building up the body of Christ,
Ephesians 4:11-12 (ESV)

If we believe that Jesus forbids us to use the term "father" in any context, why are we not equally troubled to use the term "teacher" or "Sunday School teacher"? I suspect it is because we do not have so much historical-emotional investment in the term "teacher". Therefore, we easily, if not thoughtlessly, accept Jesus' use of "teacher" in a hyperbole to make a point. Certainly, no one has ever chided me with, "Call no man teacher!" Were it not for the visceral reaction to the Roman Catholic Church during the Reformation Movement, we might not be troubled to use the term "father" when addressing a humble pastor whom we view as a member of our Christian family.

Likewise, the title "elder" (presbyter), which was used in the Early Church for the office that we call "priest" today is also found in Paul's letters to Timothy and Titus. Clearly it referred to those who were recognized as having spiritual maturity as Christians, and who were called or ordained to serve in roles of leadership in the Church. The term "father" as we use it today carries the same connotation by Christians as does "elder". Not one to be revered, but one

The Meaning and Symbols of Holy Eucharist

who has been entrusted with a measure of spiritual responsibility for the brothers and sisters in the church.

> *So I exhort the elders among you, as a fellow elder and a witness of the sufferings of Christ, as well as a partaker in the glory that is going to be revealed: shepherd the flock of God that is among you, exercising oversight, not under compulsion, but willingly, as God would have you; not for shameful gain, but eagerly; not domineering over those in your charge, but being examples to the flock. And when the chief Shepherd appears, you will receive the unfading crown of glory. Likewise, you who are younger, be subject to the elders. Clothe yourselves, all of you, with humility toward one another, for "God opposes the proud but gives grace to the humble."*
>
> 1 Peter 5:1-5 (ESV)

The fact that there were leadership roles in the Early Church is also made clear in the letter to the Hebrews.

> *Obey your leaders and submit to them, for they are keeping watch over your souls, as those who will have to give an account. Let them do this with joy and not with groaning, for that would be of no advantage to you.*
>
> Hebrews 13:17 (ESV)

This verse fills me with fear at times as I think about the account that I will have to give. And, often when someone calls me "father", I find myself praying and hoping I can live up to the role that God has called me to – whatever the title.

The Meaning and Symbols of Holy Eucharist

+

Therefore let us be grateful for receiving a kingdom that cannot be shaken, and thus let us offer to God acceptable worship, with reverence and awe, for our God is a consuming fire.

Hebrews 12.28, 29 [ESV]

+

The Meaning and Symbols of Holy Eucharist

APPENDICES

APPENDIX A.

The Prayer of Hippolytus

The Eucharistic Prayer of Hippolytus is one of the earliest known recorded Eucharistic liturgies of the ancient Church. For those who come from a non-liturgical christian denomination, it may come as something of a shock to discover that a written liturgy came this early in the history of the Church. Especially, if you were told that Eucharisitc Liturgies were the invention of medieval clergy who were biblically illiterate. Clearly, that is not the case. In fact, Hippolytus was the disciple of Irenæus, who is believed to have been a student of the Apostle John.

Consider the example of baseball: in Hoboken, New Jersey the first organized baseball game was played in 1846. 19 years later, on the very same ball field, some 20,000 people were assembled to watch a baseball game between the Mutual Club of Manhattan and the Atlantic Club of Brooklyn. When I was a child in 1965 – 100 years later – people were still playing baseball pretty much the same

The Meaning and Symbols of Holy Eucharist

way. The point is: the written evidence of these early Liturgies and their general consistency one with another, speak in favor of a continuum rather than an innovation.

The way the instructions of Hippolytus are phrased, it is apparent that he is describing something that has been going on for a while. And, this Eucharistic Liturgy does not stand in isolation. Saint Paul's corrective in First Corinthians 11.17-34 is the earliest example. And, there are similar phrases and prayers in early patristic writings, such as *The Didache* (ca. 60) and *Justin Martyr* (ca. 135), and other full Eucharistic Liturgies, such as *The Divine Liturgy of James the Holy Apostle and Brother of the Lord*; *The Divine Liturgy of the Holy Apostle and Evangelist Mark, The Disciple of the Holy Peter*; and *The Liturgy of the Blessed Apostles, composed by Saint Adæus and Saint Maris, Teachers of the Easterns*, which are third or fourth century texts. The full texts of these liturgies can be found in the Ante-Nicene Fathers, Volume 7, [Philip Schaff, Ed.]

This Eucharistic prayer comes from an early Church manual known as the *Apostolic Tradition* of Saint Hippolytus and is part of lengthier instructions relating to the consecration of a bishop. We would now refer to this as an *ordinal*. In contemporary liturgies, the consecration would be part of the first section of the celebration known as the Liturgy of the Word. What is recorded here is the second section: the Liturgy of the Table. After the bishop has been consecrated, he begins to offer his first Eucharistic celebration as a bishop. The Liturgy continues here with the Offertory (oblation), which is followed by the Sursum Corda ("Lift up your hearts").

The Eucharisitc Prayer of Hippolytus of Rome

- A.D. 215 -

When he has been made bishop, everyone shall give him the kiss of peace, and salute him respectfully, for he has been made worthy of this. Then the deacons shall present the oblation to him, and he shall lay his hand upon it, and give thanks, with the entire council of elders, saying:

The Lord be with you.

And all reply: And with your spirit.

The bishop says: Lift up your hearts.

The people respond: We have them with the Lord.

The bishop says: Let us give thanks to the Lord.

The people respond: It is proper and just.

The bishop then continues:

We give thanks to you God, through your beloved son Jesus

The Meaning and Symbols of Holy Eucharist

Christ, whom you sent to us in former times as Savior, Redeemer, and Messenger of your Will, who is your inseparable Word, through whom you made all, and in whom you were well-pleased, whom you sent from heaven into the womb of a virgin, who, being conceived within her, was made flesh, and appeared as your Son, born of the Holy Spirit and the virgin.

It is he who, fulfilling your will and acquiring for you a holy people, extended his hands in suffering, in order to liberate from sufferings those who believe in you.

Who, when he was delivered to voluntary suffering, in order to dissolve death, and break the chains of the devil, and tread down hell, and bring the just to the light, and set the limit, and manifest the resurrection, taking the bread, and giving thanks to you, said,

"Take, eat, for this is my body which is broken for you."

Likewise the chalice, saying,

This is my blood which is shed for you.
Whenever you do this, do this (in) memory of me.

Therefore, remembering his death and resurrection, we offer to you the bread and the chalice, giving thanks to you, who has made us worthy to stand before you and to serve as your priests.

And we pray that you would send your Holy Spirit to the oblation of your Holy Church. In their gathering together, give to all those who partake of your holy mysteries the fullness of the Holy Spirit, toward the strengthening of the

The Meaning and Symbols of Holy Eucharist

faith in truth, that we may praise you and glorify you, through your son Jesus Christ, through whom to you be glory and honor, Father and Son, with the Holy Spirit, in your Holy Church, now and throughout the ages of the ages. Amen.

☩

[Christ] was altogether in all, and everywhere; and though He filleth the universe up to all the principalities of the air, He stripped Himself again. And for a brief space He cries that the cup might pass from Him, with a view to show truly that He was also man. But remembering, too, the purpose for which He was sent, He fulfills the dispensation (economy) for which He was sent, and exclaims, "Father, not my will," and, "The spirit is willing, but the flesh is weak."

    St. Hippolytus, Bishop and Martyr,
    in his Homily on the Paschal Supper.

☩

APPENDIX B.

Collects and Preface

What is a COLLECT?

Collect originates from the Latin term *collecta*, which means "the *gathering of people together* as well as to the *collecting up* of the petitions of individual members of the congregation into one prayer." [*from* The Collects of Thomas Cranmer by C.F. Barbee & Paul Zahl]

Collects reflect the *theme of the day*. More so during Advent, Christmas, Lent, Easter and Saints' days, than during the Propers after Pentecost, being Ordinary Time. In Ordinary Time the theme is generally on discipleship, ministry and evangelism. The Collect, the Lessons, and the Proper Preface are all coordinated to present teaching, prayer and worship that is unified according to the season.

♦ Collects are written according to the following structure:

1. The Address
2. The Acknowledgement
3. The Petition
4. The Aspiration (does not appear in all collects – note Proper 11, below)
5. The Pleading

The Meaning and Symbols of Holy Eucharist

Example   The Collect for Purity

(1) Almighty God, (2) to you all hearts are open, all desires known, and from you no secrets are hid: (3) Cleanse the thoughts of our hearts by the inspiration of your Holy Spirit, (4) that we may perfectly love you, and worthily magnify your holy Name; (5) through Christ our Lord. *Amen.*

Example   The Collect of the Day
[See 1979 BCP, page 231, *Collects, Contemporary*]

Proper 11   *The Sunday closest to July 20*

(1) Almighty God, the fountain of all wisdom, (2) you know our necessities before we ask and our ignorance in asking: (3) Have compassion on our weakness, and mercifully give us those things which for our unworthiness we dare not, and for our blindness we cannot ask; (5) through the worthiness of your Son Jesus Christ our Lord, who lives and reigns with you and the Holy Spirit, one God, now and for ever. *Amen.*

Note: Proper 11 was originally written by Archbishop Thomas Cranmer for the 1549 Book of Common Prayer (BCP) as a closing prayer to the Liturgy of the Word, if the Eucharist was not going to follow. The scriptural antecedents for the prayer are found in Ecclesiasticus 1.5, Matthew 6:8 and Romans 8:26. This collect was included with the occasional prayers, for the Daily Office in the 1928 BCP.

The Meaning and Symbols of Holy Eucharist

Preface of the Lord's Day

The Proper Preface corresponds to the Collect and Lessons, and is included in the Eucharistic celebration between the Sursum Corda and Sanctus. [See the notes in the Instructed Eucharist, above, and 1979 BCP pages 377-382]

References: The Collects of Th. Cranmer by Barbee & Zahl, Commentary on the American Prayer Book by Hatchett, The Oxford American Prayer Book Commentary by Shepherd.

APPENDIX C.

Praying the Daily Office

The following guidelines were written for those who lead Morning Prayer in public worship. However, the guidelines will also be useful to help those praying privately navigate their way through Morning Prayer. Once you are familiar with the flow of Morning Prayer, you will see that Evening Prayer follows a similar rhythm.

Outline for Morning Prayer Rite II

With notes for a Lay Officiant, or Lay Reader.

Notes.
- Only the Office Lights are lit (and Paschal Candle in Easter; Advent candles in Advent); the Altar candles are not lit unless the Eucharist follows.
- The collect and lessons should be selected before the service begins.
- Vesting is cassock, surplice and tippet.

The Meaning and Symbols of Holy Eucharist

Morning Prayer Rite II

Begin with either (1) a Versicle [BCP 75] *or* (4) Preces [BCP 80]

1. Versicle – choose one appropriate to the season [BCP 75-78] – *standing.*

2. Confession – choose one intro [BCP 79] – *kneeling (or standing).*

3. Absolution – adjust for Lay Reader [BCP 80] – *lay officiant remains kneeling.*

Note: the "Amen" during the confession is not italicized, while the *"Amen"* at the absolution is italicized. This is a universal clue throughout the BCP indicating whether or not the people participate in the preceding prayer. If the *Amen* is italicized the officiant leads the prayer alone and the people respond with the *Amen.* Where the Amen is not italicized, the preceding prayer (or Creed) is said by all. Compare the Amen in the prayer of General Thanksgiving [BCP 101], with the *Amen* in the prayer of Saint Chrysostom [BCP 102].

4. Preces - "Lord open our lips" [BCP 80] – *standing; sign the cross over lips.*

The Invitatory and Psalter

Gloria – *standing.*

The Meaning and Symbols of Holy Eucharist

Antiphon – choose appropriate to the season [BCP 80-82] – Traditionally the antiphon is said before and after the Invitatory (Venite/Jubilate/Pascha Nostrum), with the congregation responding with "Come let us adore Him." - *standing*.

Invitatory Psalms: Venite/Jubilate/Pascha Nostrum – *standing*. *Optional:* Antiphon is repeated afterward.

Psalms – there are two methods for selecting the psalms – *seated or standing*.
  A. Choose according to the Daily Office Lectionary (BCP 934-1001). For example, Monday of First week in Advent, Year One (BCP 936) provides Psalms 1, 2, 3 for M.P. and Psalms 4, 7 for E.P.
  B. Choose according to day of the month (Benedictine practice). See the rubric above Psalm One (BCP 585), *First Day: Morning Prayer*
  Note: for either method, the psalms are offered without pause, the officiant begins each psalm (even if he/she ended the previous), the Gloria Patri is offered only once at the end of the series of psalms. The asterisk provides for a unified breath. (See rubrics: BCP 934-935). Stuhlman notes, "The psalms are traditionally recited standing in the Anglican office; sometimes, however, they are recited seated. The first alternative treats them as acts of praise; the second, following the monastic tradition, as texts for meditation." (Prayer Book Rubrics Expanded – Byron D. Stuhlman, page 38)

The Meaning and Symbols of Holy Eucharist

Gloria Patri. - *Commonly still seated after the Psalm/s, following the Benedictine tradition.*

The Lessons

Old Testament Lesson. Choose according to the Daily Office Lectionary (BCP 934-1001) *Officiant standing; people seated.*

Canticle. Note: hymns may be substituted. *Standing.*

New Testament Lesson. Choose according to the Daily Office Lectionary (BCP 934-1001). Note: commonly the Gospel lesson is left for E.P. (see "Concerning the Daily Office Lectionary" pages 934-935 for more instructions.) *Officiant standing; people seated.*

Canticle. Note: hymns may be substituted. *Standing*

Apostles Creed. *Standing.*

The Prayers

The Lord's Prayer. *Kneeling or standing.*

Suffrages – Choose A or B. (Note that Suffrages A are also offered during Evening Prayer.) "V" indicates the Officiant. "R" indicates the response. - *kneeling.*

The Meaning and Symbols of Holy Eucharist

The Collect of the Day. (1)   The collect from the Sunday of the current week may be offered. Or, the collect for a Feast Day, if there is one, may be offered. Major Feast Days (or Holy Days) are listed in bold, and Lesser Feasts and Fasts are listed in normal print on pages 19-30. The contemporary collects for Holy Days are found on pages 237-250. Specific collects for Lesser Feasts and Fasts are found in the book titled "Lesser Feasts and Fasts". However, universal collects for martyrs, missionaries, and saints are found on pages 246-250. - *kneeling.*

Collect of the Day (2) – choose from a collect appropriate to the day of the week from those listed, between *A Collect for Sundays* [98] and *A Collect for Guidance* [100].

Collect for Mission – choose one from the three listed on pages 100 and 101.

Optional: Hymn or Anthem. This is the only rubric in M.P. indicating a hymn but this is not the only place where a hymn may be sung. [BCP 101]

Optional: Homily or Devotional may be offered here. (See note: BCP 142)

Optional: Intercessions and Thanksgivings. (See rubrics on page 101, and directions on page 142.)

The Meaning and Symbols of Holy Eucharist

Optional: Offering. This is not an Offertory and should not be treated as such, since there will be no presentation at the altar, as in Communion. (See note: BCP 142). While not indicated, this is also a suitable place for announcements.

Note: The rubric zone between the Collect for Mission and the General Thanksgiving seems to be left as open territory for anything still needed in the service. The order of hymn, homily, intercessions and offering is flexible.

The General Thanksgiving. - *Officiant and people; kneeling or standing.*

The Prayer of St. Chrysostom. This prayer is not required if the General Thanksgiving has been offered. One, or both may be used (see rubric, pg. 101). [BCP 102] This prayer is indicated for the officiant, but is commonly offered by both officiant and people. – *kneeling or standing.*

Dismissal. - *standing.*

Scripture. The concluding scripture correlates to a blessing.- *standing; traditional to cross one's self..*

Glossary of Terms

Ablutions. The ritual of hand washing by the Celebrant following the Offertory. Also, the cleansing of the chalice, paten, and other vessels after administration of communion.

Acolyte. One who assists or serves the priest or deacon at the altar before, during, and after the Communion service.

Altar Book. The large book containing the text from "The Book of Common Prayer" and service music for the celebrant at the Eucharist.

Ambo. A raised pulpit or lectern.

Aumbry. Or, "Ambry". A recess or receptacle built into the wall for the Reserved Sacrament, usually located near the altar. (See tabernacle)

Baptismal Font. The basin for the administration of the Sacrament of Holy Baptism.

Burse. The pocket or envelope of stiff board covered with material of the same liturgical color as the vestments, in which the corporal is kept when not in use on the altar.

Celebrant. The principal officiant at the Eucharist and other Sacramental services. The Bishop is the ordinary celebrant, or, if the Bishop is not present, a priest.

Chalice. The "common cup" of the Lord's Supper. Typically made of costly metal, but may also be a ceramic cup, into which the wine (and a little water) is poured, to be consecrated during Holy Eucharist, and given to the congregation during Communion.

The Meaning and Symbols of Holy Eucharist

Chalice Veil. A square piece of material (of the same liturgical colors as the vestments) used to cover the chalice and paten when not in use. The burse (with the corporal & purifcator inside) rests on top of the veiled chalice.

Chasuble. A long wide sleeveless vestment, worn by the celebrant at the Eucharist. It is of the liturgical color of the day or season. The chasuble symbolizes the glory of God filling the Holy Place.

Ciborium. A covered metal or ceramic vessel in which the Blessed Sacrament is kept when reserved in a tabernacle or aumbry.

Collect. A prayer that is sung or said on behalf of the people by the celebrant or officiant at liturgical celebrations.

Cope. A long cape worn over the shoulders by the celebrant, or officiant at various liturgies (processions, burials, etc.) or by a bishop. It has a clasp at the chest and is worn over an alb and stole and other vestments, corresponding to the liturgical color of the day or season.

Corporal. A large square white cloth, usually linen, that is placed on the altar – upon which chalice and paten are placed.

Credence Table. A table, usually to the right of the altar, on which the vessels and other items for the celebration of the Eucharist are kept.

Crucifer. One who carries the Processional Cross and usually leads the procession.

The Meaning and Symbols of Holy Eucharist

Cruets. Glass or metal containers with stoppers and handles for the wine and water. They are usually found on the Credence Table.

Dalmatic. A tunic worn by the Deacon of the Mass. Usually, it is ornate and corresponds in color and fabric to the chasuble worn by the Celebrant.

Doxology. Words said or sung in praise of the Holy Trinity.

Elements. The bread and wine to be consecrated at the Eucharist.

Eucharistic Candles. Two candles placed on the altar, at each end of the altar. As you face the altar with your back to the Nave, the one on the right is known as the "Epistle Candle" and one on the left is known as the "Gospel Candle". They are lit before each Eucharistic Service and extinguished at the end of the service. The Epistle Candle should be lit first and extinguished last, if only the two candles are used. The Gospel Candle "never stands alone."

Flagon. A large glass or metal container often used for wine to be consecrated at the Eucharist, if more than one chalice is used during the administration of communion.

Fermentum. Early Church: A piece of consecrated bread sent by one bishop to another bishop as an expression of unity (ie. Communion). Now: some diocesan bishops will send a piece of consecrated bread to churches within his diocese to be added to the chalice on Maundy Thursday as an expression of diocesan unity.

Font. Generally, a large basin near the entrance of the church where baptisms are conducted. The font may be kept filled with water at other times, so that people may dip their fingers, making the sign of the cross to recall their

The Meaning and Symbols of Holy Eucharist

baptismal vows. Otherwise, the font is filled with water and blessed during the baptismal Liturgy.

Genuflection. The bending of the right knee when reverencing the Blessed Sacrament.

Instructed Eucharist. Typically a celebration of the Eucharist where the Liturgy is paused at certain moments while the celebrant, or a narrator, provides instruction for that portion of the Liturgy.

Intinction. A way of administration of elements of communion by dipping the bread in the consecrated wine and placing on the tongue of the one receiving Communion.

Lavabo. The table or niche where a pitcher, bowl and towel set are used for washing the celebrant's fingers after the Offertory at the Eucharist, or at other times such as when oil or chrism is used.

Lavabo Bowl. The metal or ceramic dish into which the water is poured by the server at the lavabo, for the ablutions. Where churches do not have a separate lavabo, these items are generally placed on the credence table.

Lavabo Towel. A piece a cloth presented to the celebrant by the server to dry his fingers during the ablutions.

Lay Reader. (Or, simply "Reader.") One who is licensed to officiate at the Daily Offices and other non-sacramental prayer book services. A Licensed Lay Reader should not be confused with a "Lector" (See below).

Lectern. The Book-stand or podium from which the lessons and sometimes the Gospel are read at the Eucharist and other offices. Also called an Ambo.

The Meaning and Symbols of Holy Eucharist

Lector. A person who reads the lessons at the Liturgy. (Not to be confused with a Lay Reader.)

Liturgy. The "work of the people." In Western usage this term may apply to any public celebration of the Church. In the Churches of the East, the Divine Liturgy refers specifically to the celebration of the Holy Eucharist. When capitalized, the *Liturgy* refers to the Holy Eucharist. Printed in lower case letters, *liturgy* refers to any worship service following a recognized structure.

Narthex. An area or entry way between the outer doors of the church and the inner doors of the Nave. This has the practical benefit of having a location to hang coats and pick-up useful literature, while maintaining silence within the Nave. The Narthex is also a traditional location for the font, as a way of visually and practically demonstrating that we enter the Church through Holy Baptism.

Nave. The area in the church where people are gathered for the liturgy. Traditional architecture may reflect a ceiling that has beams reminiscent of the interior of a ship. This is no accident, as the Church Fathers thought of the Church as the Ark that brings us to salvation. [Compare 1 Peter 3:18-21]

Office Lights. The six candles- three on each side of the cross which are lighted for the Daily Office -- the liturgical services for the order of daily prayers, (Morning and Evening Prayer.) They are also used at a Sung Eucharist, and on certain services for special days.

Pall. A stiffened square of linen (or Other) white cloth that is placed over the chalice to keep objects from falling into the wine. The term may also refer to the cloth covering the casket or urn during the Burial of the Dead.

The Meaning and Symbols of Holy Eucharist

Paschal Candle. A large decorated (with a cross and Alpha and Omega letters) placed in a holder in the north side of the sanctuary and lighted at all services throughout Eastertide. It is also lighted near the Baptismal Font when there is a Baptism in the Church.

Paten. A metal or ceramic plate on which the bread is placed for consecration and from which the consecrated bread is administered at the Holy Communion

Pavement Lights. Large white candles in candlestand which stands on the floor, one on each side of front of the altar. These may be the same candles as the Torches carried by acolytes in procession.

Pectoral Cross. A large cross worn by a bishop.

Piscina. A sink for washing the vessels used at the Eucharist and for reverently disposing of wine that has been consecrated. The piscina does not drain into the sewer or a disposal system, but directly to the ground.

Pre-Sanctified. See, "Reserve Sacrament".

Processional Cross. A metal or wooden cross affixed to a pole and carried in processions by the Crucifer.

Pulpit. The place from which the sermon is preached and from which the Gospel may be read.

Purificator. A fine linen (or other) white cloth used for wiping the chalice during the administration of Communion and for cleansing the paten and chalice during ablutions.

The Meaning and Symbols of Holy Eucharist

Pyx. A portable container for carrying the Blessed Host. A pyx is usually made of fine metal with decoration on the lid, secured with a clasp and hinged to open at the top. Clergy use it to take Communion in one-kind to the sick. Licensed Lay Ministers will present a pyx at the Altar on an assigned Sunday to carry the Blessed Sacrament to the chronically ill and home bound. A pyx may be placed inside a corresponding pouch that hangs from the neck so that others may recognize that Jesus is being borne to the sick.

Requiem Mass. A Mass with music for the repose of souls.

Reserve Sacrament. The Consecrated Bread and Wine reserved in the Tabernacle/Aumbry for administration to the sick or others who are not able attend the celebration of the Eucharist. Also referred to as the "Pre-sanctified."

Sanctuary Candle. A clear/translucent container with a candle that burns near the place where the Blessed Sacrament is reserved. The candle is never extinguished when the Sacrament is present.

Sacristy. A room where the vessels, vestments, and other liturgical objects are kept, and also may be the room where the clergy and assistants vest before the Liturgy, (where there is no separate vestry room). See "Vestry".

Sanctuary. The area of the church surrounding the altar.

Sanctus Bell. A bell or set of bells sometimes called Sacred Bell because it is rung at the time of the Sanctus, the "Holy, Holy, Holy, and may be rung to call attention to the Consecration of the bread and wine. In some churches it is rung at the elevations of the consecrated elements by the Celebrant.

The Meaning and Symbols of Holy Eucharist

Sedillia. Seats for the clergy, lay ministers and acolytes in the Sanctuary.

Stole. A long strip of cloth or material used by bishops, priests, and deacons when officiating at the Eucharist or other sacramental functions. It is worn over the alb and is of the liturgical color of the day or season.

Tabernacle. A box or house-shaped receptacle for the Reserved Sacrament located on or near the altar. (See Aumbry)

Torchbearer. Acolytes who carry the torches or processional candles, one on each side of the Processional Cross.

Vestry. The "vestry" commonly refers to the group of lay leaders responsible for the ongoing needs and ministry of a parish. However, the "vestry" also refers to the room where the clergy vest.

Acknowledgments

This book began as a response to numerous requests for a live "Instructed Eucharist" which I find incompatible with genuine worship. Originally, I wrote a small booklet that people could pick up as they entered the church building to act as a quick reference guide for those unfamiliar with liturgical worship, and those who wanted an Instructed Eucharist. Over time that booklet grew into the book you now hold.

Much of the teaching and observations about worship and the Liturgy contained in these pages are the result of priestcraft – traditions, principles and wisdom that are passed down from bishops, priests and deacons who mentor seminarians and recently ordained priests. I was tremendously blessed to have numerous mentors who loved the Lord and had years of experience as deacons, priests and bishops that they shared freely with me and others. The gratitude that I feel for the following clergymen is beyond quantification:

The Right Reverend John-David Schofield, R.I.P.
The Reverend Gregory Waddington, R.I.P.
The Reverend Deacon Elmer Gould, R.I.P.
The Reverend Canon James Thompson
The Very Reverend Carlos Raines
The Right Reverend Eric Vawter Menees
The Right Reverend Alberto Morales, O.S.B.

I am also greatly indebted to my wife, Jacqueline, who was (and is) consistently encouraging me to write because she knows it brings me so much satisfaction. I also appreciate the early encouragement that I received from Mrs. Mary K Leonard, the Altar Guild Directress of Saint James' Cathedral in the Diocese of San Joaquin. The Reverend Dale Matson was my go-to-guy for understanding the mechanics of self-publication and what I needed to do to move from a booklet on a photocopier to a real bound book. Mrs. Sarah "Sally" Karlowicz gave much of her time to reading through the book numerous times to offer advice and corrections. Her suggestions and corrections have added much to the finished quality of the book. (Any remaining errors or goofs are my fault not hers!).

Best of all: thanks be to God for giving us so many beautiful ways to worship!

Bibliography

The Anglican Service Book [1979 in Traditional English, with supplements]. The Church of the Good Shepherd, Rosemont, Pennsylvania, 1991.

Ante-Nicene Fathers, Volume 5. Edited by Philip Schaff

Ante-Nicene Fathers, Volume 7. Edited by Philip Schaff

The Barnhart Concise Dictionary of Etymology, by Robert K. Barnhart, Harper Collins, NY, 1995

The Book of Common Prayer [1662]. Introduction by Diarmaid MacCulloch, Everyman's Library, 1999

The Book of Common Prayer [1928]. The Church Pension Fund, NY, 1945.

The Book of Common Prayer [1979]. Oxford University Press, NY, 2007.

The Book of Occasional Services. Church Publishing Incorporated, NY

The Catechetical Lectures of Saint Cyril of Jerusalem, Kindle

The Collects of Thomas Cranmer. Compiled by C. Frederick Barbee and Paul F. M. Zahl, Eerdmans Publishing, 1999

Common Worship. Church House Publishing, London, 2000.

Commentary on the American Prayer Book [1979]. by Marion Hatchett, Seabury Press, NY, 1981

The Meaning and Symbols of Holy Eucharist

Daily Office Book – Year One/Year Two [1979]. Church Publishing, NY.

Early Christian Fathers. Translated and edited by Cyril C. Richardson, The Westminster Press, Philadelphia, 1953.

The First English Prayer Book [1549]. by Thomas Cranmer (Ed. by Robert Van de Weyer), Morehouse Publishing, Harrisburg PA, 1999

From the Fathers to the Churches: Daily Spiritual Readings. Edited by Brother Kenneth, Collins Liturgical Publications, London, 1988.

Handbook of Prayers, ed. James Socias, Princeton, NJ: Sceptor Publishers, 1997

The Holy Bible, English Standard Version. by Crossway Bibles, a division of Good News Publishers, Wheaton, IL, 2001.

Interlinear Greek New Testament Bible, by Frederick Scrivener and Henry Ambrose, Kindle

www.justus.anglican.org (this website provides a great number of resources.)

Lesser Feasts and Fasts [1997]. Church Publishing Incorporated, NY

My Prayer-Book – Happiness in Goodness – Reflections, Counsels, Prayers, and Devotions. Lasance, F.L., NY: Benziger Brothers, 1944

The Navarre Bible: The Psalms and the Song of Solomon. By University of Navarre, Sceptor Publishers, NY, 2003

Nicene and Post-Nicene Fathers, Series II, Volume 3.
Edited by Philip Schaff

Nicene and Post-Nicene Fathers, Series II, Volume 7.
Edited by Philip Schaff

Nicene and Post-Nicene Fathers, Series II, Volume 10.
Edited by Philip Schaff

The Oxford American Prayer Book Commentary [1928], by Massey Hamilton Shepherd, Oxford University Press, NY, 1973

The Oxford Dictionary of the Christian Church. (2nd Ed.) Edited by F.L. Cross and E.A. Livingstone, Oxford University Press, Great Britain, 1974

The Oxford Guide to the Book of Common Prayer – A Worldwide Survey. Ed. by Chs Hefling and Cynthia Shattuck, Oxford University Press, 2006

The Practice of Religion – A Short Manual of Instructions and Devotions. by Archibald Campbell Knowles, Morehouse-Gorham Co. NY, 1950

The Prayer Book Office. Compiled by Howard Galley, The Seabury Press, 1980

Prayers of the Eucharist – Early and Reformed. by R.C.D. Jasper & G.J. Cuming, The Liturgical Press, Collinsville, Minnesota, 1980

Readings for the Daily Office from the Early Church. Ed. by J. Robert Wright, Church Hymnal Corporation, NY, 1991

The Meaning and Symbols of Holy Eucharist

Saint Augustine's Prayer Book – A Book of Devotions for Members of the Episcopal Church [1947]. Ed. by Loren Gavitt, Holy Cross Publications, West Park, NY, 1999

Serving Basics. The Order of Saint Vincent.

Theology and Sanity. by Frank Sheed, Ignatius Press, San Francisco, 1993.

They Still Speak – Readings for the Lesser Feasts. Ed. by J. Robert Wright, Church Hymnal Corporation, NY, 1993

Thomas Cranmer. by Arthur James Mason, Metheun & Co., London, 1898

Voices of the Saints – A Year of Readings. by Bert Ghezzi, Doubleday, NY, 2000

Worshipping the Lord in the Anglican Way. [1928 BCP in Contemporary English]. Preservation Press of the Prayerbook Society, USA, 2005

The Meaning and Symbols of Holy Eucharist

Contact:

Much of this study guide was written from memory; the oral tradition of priestcraft passed down to me from my mentors. I confess that in my eagerness to publish it, I may not have caught some errors. If you discover errors, or have any other comments – including matters regarding your personal faith and relationship with Christ that you wish to explore, please contact the author at

Saint Austin's Desk
info@austinspress.com
or
Fr. Van McCalister
fr.mccalister@gmail.com

Printed in Great Britain
by Amazon